The Basics of

Collecting

MONEY

Written by
Paul Gilkes
COIN WORLD Staff Writer

**COIN WORLD staff also contributing to this book:
Beth Deisher, William T. Gibbs, P. Bradley Reed**

Published by Amos Press Inc., Post Office Box 150, Sidney, Ohio 45365.
Publishers of Coin World, the weekly newspaper of the entire numismatic field; Linn's Stamp News, the world's largest weekly stamp newspaper; Cars and Parts, the magazine serving the car hobbyist; and the Scott publishing line of philatelic catalogs and albums.

This book is available at special quantity discounts for bulk
purchases.
For details, write Amos Press Inc.
Coin World Products
P.O. Box 150, Sidney, Ohio 45365
or call (513) 498-0800

ISBN: 0-944945-03-1

Library of Congress Catalog Card Number: 89-84282

Contents

Getting started

Question: How many sides does a coin have?

Answer: Would you be surprised that the answer is "three"?

Everyone recognizes the "heads and tails" of a coin, what coin collectors refer to as "**obverse** and **reverse**." The third side is the **edge**. The edge of a coin may have its own design. It can be plain, like a cent, or reeded, like a dime, or have any variation of lettering or designs.

Just as there are more sides to a coin than you might expect, so are there more sides to the hobby of collecting money than may be obvious at first glance.

Coin collecting is just one small part of the broader field of

numismatics (pronounced noo-miz-ma-ticks) — the science, study or collecting of coins, tokens, medals, orders and decorations, paper money, primitive money and related items.

Under the broader umbrella of numismatics is crowded every medium of exchange used by man for more than 2,600 years; whether it be an animal's tooth, a bronze necklace, official coinage issues in various metals, or paper currency, from nations around the world.

People also collect unofficial money substitutes, such as **tokens**, which are accepted for use

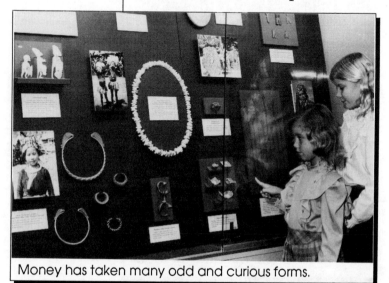

Money has taken many odd and curious forms.

in commerce and trade in exchange for goods and services.

The umbrella of numismatics also covers items produced in a manner similar to the production of money. **Medals**, produced in a wide range of materials in a variety of shapes and designs, may picture subjects to honor a nation's statesmen, to commemorate a sports event, or provide for the engraver an outlet for creating original designs. Many people collect medals designed or engraved by artists who also design coins.

A similar range of fields is open to collectors of paper money. Collectibles range from official issues of governments, to special-use issues such as military scrip or emergency money, to privately issued notes. Many paper money collectors also collect **souvenir cards** or **vignettes** which are produced in a manner similar to the manufacture of paper money, or which may depict the artistry of paper money engravers.

And under the umbrella of numismatics is the very popular

THE TERM "EXONUMIA" refers to collectible items that are related to money, either by function, method of production or other means.

field of collecting error coins and paper money. Much of the appeal of error coins and notes is in their curiosity. But much can be learned about the manufacturing process by examining certain error pieces. More will be explained about the manufacturing process in a later section.

Collecting money and related items can appeal to people of any social or economic background.

There are almost as many reasons for collecting money as there are collectors. To some, their collections are primarily financial investments. Most collectors, however, while keenly aware of the financial worth of their collections, have additional motives for collecting.

Coins and other numismatic items give us a valuable perspective on the cultures that create and use them. From a historical point of view, coins depict statesmen, athletes, scientists, and even mythological characters. Even the denominations of coins, the metals used in producing them, and

THE FIRST COINS are generally thought to have been invented in Lydia in Asia Minor around 650 B.C.

the methods by which they are produced convey a great deal of historical information.

Some coins are "souvenirs" of ancient times that we can hold in our hands. By collecting and studying them, we can learn what ancient people considered valuable,

Ancient coins such as these tell us much about their makers.

what symbols or ideals were important to them, and the sophistication of their artists. In many cases, portraits engraved on coins are the only remaining images of the ceasars, emperors and kings of lands that now are little more than legend.

Paper money, too, is crowded with information about its people. Look at a note from a foreign land. You can get a feeling for the language, the artistic style, the cultural symbols of people you may never meet face to face. What do you think people in other countries can learn about us from looking at our money?

Washington first appeared on the quarter in 1932, the bicentennial of his birth.

Look through the money in your pocket or purse. Have you ever wondered how it is made? Who decides what "pictures" or designs appear on our money? How did the likenesses of Presidents Lincoln, Washington, Jefferson, Roosevelt and Kennedy come to be on the coins we use today? Who created these likenesses? What is the purpose of the detailed engraving on our paper money? What is the meaning of the eye above the pyramid on the back of a dollar bill?

When you start asking yourself questions like these, and when you have the proper tools to find the answers, then you are well on your way toward graduating from mere accumulator of interesting items to becoming a true numismatist.

All these approaches to coin collecting and more are reflected in a rich tradition of numismatic literature. Entire libraries exist of thousands of books and other publications devoted to numismatics. Many collectors find as much enjoyment browsing through numismatic libraries as in collecting. At the same time, you need not be overwhelmed by this mass of learning. A few well-chosen reference works will provide the basic information needed for well-informed collecting. And having the book in hand can make a world of difference in the development of your collecting habits. A famous New York numismatist, Aaron Feldman, once said, "Buy the book before the coin." It makes sense.

SOME PEOPLE collect books as well as coins. They are called "bibliophiles."

Who was the first coin collector? No one really knows. Once considered a hobby for the wealthy and powerful, coin collecting has developed into a popular pastime for people in all walks of life.

You will certainly find it worthwhile to join a local coin club in your area where coin collectors with varied collecting interests can share their knowledge in, and enjoyment of, their specialized areas of collecting. Joining a coin club can provide you with information about other areas of material to collect that you may never have previously considered. If there isn't a coin club in your area, you may want to start one.

Sports figures on medals is a popular collecting area.

Your own interests and curiosity will guide you in what you decide to collect. You may want to concentrate on collecting **obsolete paper money** issued by banks that once thrived in the area in which you live. You may want to collect sports medals because you like sports. At least one collector we know collects transportation tokens because his grandfather worked as a train engineer.

The amount of money and time you spend on coin collecting depends not only on the area in which you want to specialize, but on how deeply you want to be involved. And as you become more involved, you will find you share similar interests with like-minded collectors.

For those who don't have money to burn, it would be unwise to spend a fortune trying to assemble a set of United States gold coins. If money is limited, you may want to start out conservatively by going to your local bank and buying $5 worth of Lincoln cents and trying to put together a set of dates and Mint marks.

Coins can be collected according to date and the Mint mark, and can be placed in various kinds of coin folders available on the market today.

This method, followed by many beginning collectors, can provide you with hours of collecting enjoyment as you assemble, without too much trouble, a set of Lincoln cents with Lincoln Memorial reverse.

You may also find some "Wheat Ear" reverse issues the same way. The Lincoln Memorial

MINT MARKS can be letters, numbers or symbols. They may appear on either side of a coin, and identify the Mint at which the coin was struck.

Lincoln got a new reverse in 1959, his 150th birthday.

reverse refers to the Lincoln Memorial pictured on the "tails" side of the cent from 1959 until the present. A **Wheat Ear** cent or "Wheatie" refers to the ears of wheat pictured on the reverse of the Lincoln cent from its introduction in 1909 until 1959, when it was replaced by the Lincoln Memorial reverse.

COPPER-NICKEL replaced silver in United States coins when the silver content of the coins became more valuable than the face value.

Many collectors recall the days when rare and scarce silver coins (dated before 1965 when copper-nickel clad coinage was first struck) could be found in pocket change. While **clad coins** — those made of a base metal such as copper and layered with a more valuable metal — have not generated as much fervor as their silver ancestors, it would be quite an accomplishment if you could assemble a complete set of perfectly struck dimes, quarter dollars and half dollars, from 1965 to date.

The most dedicated collector usually won't spend more for a particular issue than he expects to get back when he sells his collection. Even though certain series have experienced ups and downs in recent years, collections have continued to appreciate in value as time passes, and collectors have enjoyed the results, regardless of the motives for assembling their collections in the first place.

THE FLYING EAGLE CENT of 1857-1858 was made of copper-nickel.

Although these collecting suggestions offer you little more financial reward than the face value of the coins being saved, they can provide valuable learning experiences for the beginning collector.

While hands-on experience is important and helpful, buying that first reference book covering your collecting interests is just as important. Research not only provides you with knowledge of world history, but also with the art and technology that goes into producing a specific numismatic item.

As with the collector, the investor must do more than just acquaint himself with the coins he plans to buy. He may have to learn much more to become familiar with how well the coins he plans to purchase have performed in the marketplace so he can maximize his investment. Nowadays, the investor and collector are often one.

A GOOD WAY to obtain foreign money is to ask friends who travel to bring some back for you.

Once you've had your collecting appetite whetted, where do you go to have your collecting interests satisfied?

Earlier, we suggested going to your local bank and buying $5 worth of Lincoln cents to begin assembling a collection. We also talked about the days, less than 25 years ago, when silver coins were readily available in circulation.

What if your interests lie in those silver coins, in early copper coins, world coins or paper money? Where are those kinds of numismatic collectibles found?

The number of places where you can buy coins and other numismatic items to start building your collection is endless. Possibilities include buying and trading with members at your local coin club; your local coin shop; mail order from advertisements in numismatic publications; mail-bid and public auctions; electronic teletypewriter trading and auctions; local coin shows and major coin conventions; professional numismatists; and government Mints.

IT MAY BE EASIER to buy coins than it is to sell them. Ask your dealer about his purchasing policies.

You may also find success at estate auctions, and sometimes even at flea markets.

The key to successful coin collecting is knowledge. Know what you are looking for and what you are willing to pay.

Let's start with your local coin club. Your local coin club provides members the opportunity for trading and selling duplicate items from their collection. Clubs often hold monthly auctions whereby members sell coins and other numismatic items they no longer want because either they have duplicates, they've upgraded

IF AN AUCTION LOT is available for inspection before the auction, you probably will not be able to return it if you are unsatisfied — know what you are buying!

the item they want to sell with a better example for their own collection, or their collecting tastes have changed.

Often, each item put into these auctions costs only a few dollars, allowing everyone an inexpensive chance to obtain something new to add to their collection or to start a new collection. Such auctions are also a good means of gaining the interest of young collectors.

Your local coin dealer can also be very helpful. The dealer often has expertise in more than one area of numismatics, and can provide collecting tips. In addition to coins and other numismatic material, coin shops usually offer coin collecting reference books, coin holders, and other related accessories to make assemblage of a collection more organized, yet highly enjoyable.

Larger department stores in major cities may also have a professionally staffed numismatic department.

Some coin dealers participate in one or more electronic trading networks which allow the dealer to access, by computer or teletypewriter, coins being offered by other dealers. These networks also provide you, the collector or investor, with another means of locating the specific coin or coins you want, in the condition you want, at a price you're willing to pay.

Coin World, along with other numismatic newspapers and magazines, offers classified advertisements of numismatic material offered for sale through the mail. The classifieds are broken down into various collecting categories, from Lincoln cents to gold double eagles, from scarce and rare issues to common date offerings, Proof and Uncirculated Mint sets, paper money, and tokens and medals, among others.

You will also usually find, either in the classifieds or larger display ads, coins and other material offered for sale through electronic teletypewriter and computer trading, mail-bid, and public auctions. Dealers and individuals with computer or teletypewriter access to the subscribed services can do their trad-

BESIDES BEING a good place to find coins for sale, hobby publications can keep you informed of developments that could affect your collection.

ing, buying and selling without leaving their home or business.

Some auctions are also conducted by computer access.

Bidding by mail and public auctions can be offered separately, but sometimes together. Coin companies usually print a list of the material they will be offering — either by mail-bid, public auction, or both, with appropriate deadlines for the mail-bid option — in various numismatic publications or in fliers sent directly to regular customers.

MANY COLLECTORS establish longtime friendships through mail transactions.

These listings generally include the coin company's description of the coin or other items, the grade or condition of the item based on the company's assessment, and sometimes an estimated selling price or minimum bid price.

On sales that are strictly mail-bid, bidders send in a list of the coins they are bidding on and the price they want to pay. If yours is the highest bid on a particular coin, you have the "won" the right to buy that particular coin for the winning bid price.

However, read the guidelines

and conditions for bidding and buying. Most dealers print their guidelines with the list of material offered. Some add a buyer's fee, often 10 percent of the winning bid, to the total purchase price as their commission. Some have buy-back policies in case you're not satisfied or think the item is not as described. Carefully read the conditions for bidding.

The larger coin auction companies not only advertise in various coin newspapers and periodicals, but also publish large, descriptive and extensively-illustrated catalogs of all the material being put on the auction block. The catalogs can be purchased from the various companies and are usually sent free to regular customers. The catalogs also list dates and locations of the actual public auction as well as those for viewing the items, or lots being offered.

Public viewing of the lots gives you, the potential bidder, the opportunity to look over the material to see if the material as described in the catalog meets

COIN AUCTION CATALOGS sometimes become collectibles in their own rights.

IF AN AUCTION LOT has a "reserve bid," that means it may be withdrawn from the auction if the bidding does not go high enough.

your requirements. The auctions are then run like any other auction you may have attended. The lot goes to the highest bidder, and again, a buyer's fee is usually added to the "**hammer price**" or winning bid.

Some sales combine mail bidding with the public auction. Mail bidders compete with the public, or floor bidders, for the various auction lots. In most instances, the winning bid "goes to the floor" because by being in attendance you can experience the excitement of bidding, plus have the advantage of knowing what the mail bids are.

Some sales allow a mail bidder to register a preferred bid but also include a maximum price he is willing to pay. In this case, the bidder trusts the auctioneer to increase the bid up to the approved level, if necessary, so that the bidder may win the lot.

Some mail-bid sales allow you to bid on many lots, but specify a maximum total amount you wish to spend. Some mail-bid sales will also reduce the winning bid to a percentage above the second-highest bid. These are encouragements to bid boldly on lots you may want, but if someone else also bids high on the same lot, you may end up paying more than you bargained for! You can see why it is important to read and understand the rules for each mail-bid sale.

Estate auctions and flea markets may also offer numismatic material. However, flea markets are not often staffed by professional numismatists and the material offered at estate auctions may not have been examined by a professional numismatist.

While estate auctions and flea markets can give you immediate access to numismatic material, be sure to examine the items carefully. Coins and related items sold at estate auctions and flea markets can be vastly over-priced. In some cases, you may find yourself getting a bargain. Again, knowledge is important.

Local coin shows and major coin conventions provide an arena for you to make contacts with coin dealers from your area or

REMEMBER THAT in an auction, you are not bidding against the market value of the item, but against what another bidder is willing to pay.

The coin show bourse has material for every collector.

from around the country. The dealers may specialize in U.S. coins, paper money, gold and silver bullion, tokens, world coins, or offer a wide range of numismatic items.

The **bourse**, or sales floor of the coin show or convention, whether it's a 20-table show or a major convention of 150 or more tables, is the best place to start building your collection. You can even do a little dealing yourself.

The contacts you make on the bourse, whether coin dealers or other collectors, add to your knowledge of the hobby. You may want to look for dealers on the bourse who specialize in your area of collecting and who can help you select the coins you want for your collection and locate the hard-to-find pieces.

Many dealers are willing to take the time to talk with you, sharing their knowledge of a particular coin issue and offering collecting tips. Remember, most dealers on the bourse started out just like you, a beginning collector, before jumping into numismatics as a business.

Depending on your collecting habits, you may also want to consider "the source": government Mints or Treasuries.

The United States Mint is the arm of the Treasury Department responsible for manufacturing U.S. coins. Of course, its primary function is to produce coins for everyday circulation. But it also finds time to produce special pieces for collectors.

When directed by the United States Congress, the Mint offers limited-edition commemorative coins and medals in various metals and in a wide range of prices, from a few dollars to several hundred dollars each. Recent

ONE ADVANTAGE to being on the U.S. Mint's mailing list is that you may receive pre-issue discount offers for some programs.

commemorative coins have commemorated the 1989 Bicentennial of the Congress and the 1988 Olympic Games. It has been the recent practice of Congress to attach a **surcharge** to the price of these commemoratives, which is paid to a worthy organization, such as the United States Olympic Committee for the Olympic commemorative program, or channeled directly to the United States Treasury.

The United States Mint offers many collectible items, such as this Uncirculated Mint set.

From time to time, Congress awards gold medals to deserving individuals, and sometimes authorizes the Mint to sell bronze duplicates to the public. Less often, the Mint is authorized to strike medals to be sold by another organization, such as is the case with the Young Astronauts Council.

The Mint also manufactures and sells Uncirculated Mint sets and Proof sets to collectors. An **Uncirculated Mint set** is an official set containing one coin of each currently produced denomination from each of the Mints in operation. The coins are carefully handled and packaged.

In a **Proof set,** the coins are specially manufactured from cleaned and polished planchets, or blanks, using chrome-plated dies on special low-speed, multiple-strike presses. Proof coin manufacturing is very specialized. Most of the Proof coins currently produced by the United States Mint are produced by a single facility — the San Francisco Mint. And almost all of the coining capacity of the San Francisco Mint is devoted to Proof coin prduction.

Either directly through the mail or through official distributors, collectors can buy foreign material from the source.

The government Mints of

Canada and Great Britain produce much of the world's coins, including coins specially produced for collectors. A coin issued for, say, the Bahamas was probably produced by the British Royal Mint in Llantrissant, Wales.

You may wish to receive regular mailings about coins available from various government Mints. Because so many nations do not produce their own coins, just a few mailing lists will allow you to watch for coins of many nations. Here are some starting points:

U.S. Mint, Customer Service
10001 Aerospace Road
Lanham, Md. 20706.

Royal Canadian Mint
P.O. Box 457, Station A
Ottawa, Ontario K1N 8V5
    Canada

British Royal Mint
c/o Barclay's Bank of New York
    N.A.
P.O. Box 2570
New York, N.Y. 10163.

If your interest is in world coins or paper money, and you want to know how to write for information, *Coin World* maintains a list of sources. Write and specify the country or countries you are interested in to:

Coin World
How to Order Foreign Coins
P.O. Box 150
Sidney, Ohio 45365

Paper money collectors can also receive information from the source. To get on the mailing list of The Bureau of Engraving and Printing, the branch of the Treasury Department that prints stamps, paper money, souvenir cards and other paper numismatic items, write:

Office of External Affairs
Room 533M
Bureau of Engraving and Printing
14th and C Streets, SW
Washington, D.C. 20228.

The American Bank Note Co. prints paper money for many countries. It also produces printed items specially made for collectors. Write to:

American Bank Note Co.
20 N. Airmont Road
Suffern, N.Y. 10901

If you don't have time to do the searching, but have the money, you may want to consider employing the services of a professional numismatist. Keep in mind that you're paying for the numismatist's expertise and time. The professional numismatist will, for a fee, assemble a collection according to your specifications.

As your agent, the professional numismatist will travel to coin shops, shows and conventions, look at hundreds of coins, and check the teletypewriter and computer coin-trading networks in search of those coins you want.

As you can see, there are a multitude of sources of numismatic material to start or add to your collection. Pick the ones that best suit you.

Origins of money

Before the advent of money in the form of coins, and later notes, transactions were accomplished through simple **barter**. Anything of value could be traded for something else of value. Work could be exchanged for food, food could be traded for clothing, clothing could be swapped for blankets.

Clearly prehistoric humans survived, and in some instances thrived, without money. But the advantages of a common "currency" are so strong that societies have made use of all sorts of things to serve the purpose — various metals, stones, tobacco, shells, even woodpecker scalps. In parts of Europe at the close of

EXPLORER MARCO POLO in his travels to China found salt cakes being used as money.

World War II, when many local economies had collapsed, cigarettes took on the function of money for a brief period.

The advantage of a commonly acceptable currency is one of convenience. In a simple barter system, a farmer who owns excess grain but needs baskets must find a basketweaver who needs grain. Then the farmer trades a portion of his grain for some of the basketweaver's wares.

In a complex barter system, the farmer could trade his grain for furs, then trade the furs for baskets. Money is an outgrowth of complex bartering. Instead of finding a commodity to trade, the farmer could sell his grain for cash, then pay the basketweaver cash for baskets. That way, if the basketweaver had no need of grain or of furs, he would still have an incentive to trade with the farmer — baskets for money.

When the basketweaver has a need for some commodity, he can then take the cash he got from the farmer to buy whatever he needs.

As money is passed from hand

to hand, it is said to **circulate**. We are so familiar with a cash economy that we find it difficult to imagine life without money. But try to picture modern life in a barter economy. For instance, if you needed a pair of shoes, you would have to seek out a shoemaker who has need of some service or product you could provide. You would haggle about how many hours of floor-sweeping it would take for him to provide you with a pair of shoes.

How many steps would it take for you to trade labor for the materials to manufacture, say, a bicycle? Money makes complex economies possible.

PLAYING CARDS were first used as money in Canada in the 17th century.

Designs on coins may be traced back to ancient times, in the period where lumps of metal were being transformed into coinage as we recognize it today. Small pieces of valuable metals, such as gold, silver or copper, were being traded in complex barter systems. They were traded by weight. The shekel, for instance, is recognized today as a denomination of money. But in ancient times, "shekel" was a specified weight of silver.

As trade came more and more to cross cultural bounds, the purity of the metals came to be questioned. If one culture's little gold lumps had more pure gold than another culture's little gold lumps, then the first's were more valuable for the same weight. Some money issuers began stamping a symbol of the culture as an assurance of the quality of the little gold lumps. These symbols grew into fully developed designs, and coinage as we know it was born.

THE DIFFERENCE between the cost of making a coin and its face value is called "seigniorage."

Money systems almost always become **debased**. That means that over time, their **face value** exceeds their **intrinsic value,** or the value of the metal that makes up the coin. The coins of the United States are the sizes they are because at one time their intrinsic metal value was roughly equal to their face value. Quarters and dimes were made of silver; cents were made of copper. In the history of United States coinage, you will find many sizes of coins, almost always beginning large and becoming smaller and lighter for the same face value.

Modern coins of the United States are extremely debased. The value of the copper and nickel in an Anthony dollar, Kennedy half dollar or Washington quarter is about 3 cents, far below their face values. Cents are now composed of a light plating of copper over a core of zinc. The metal value of a cent is far less than 1 cent.

Debasement is **inflationary**. Inflation means it takes more money to buy the same thing. Older readers will remember when gasoline was less than 30 cents per gallon. Younger readers will be amazed (and amused) to learn the seemingly small wages earned by their grandfathers.

Both coins have a face value of 1 cent, but the older coin is three times heavier, reflecting a change in a currency's purchasing power.

Paper money developed with the banking industry. Banks as safe depositories for coinage or precious metals began issuing slips of paper testifying that a certain amount of money was being held.

Traders found that it was very convenient to merely trade the slips of paper, rather than go to the bank and withdraw the actual metal.

In the United States, **silver certificates** promising to pay the bearer in silver coin from the U.S. Treasury were issued as late as 1963. While still legal tender, they may no longer be redeemed for silver coin.

Paper money not backed by physical reserves of coinage or precious metal, or **specie**, is called **fiat** currency. "Fiat" comes from a Latin term meaning "let it be done." In other words, fiat money

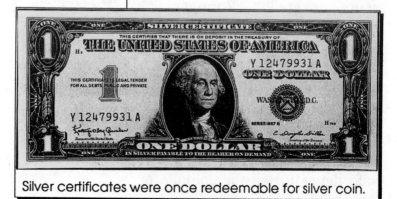

Silver certificates were once redeemable for silver coin.

is worth something simply because the government says it is, not because it represents any actual store of wealth.

The concept of **legal tender** is one that many collectors will come across. It is sometimes misunderstood, and is sometimes

Legal tender has an official OK.

times abused or misused. Basically, legal tender is officially recognized money. In other words, a ruling body has decreed that certain kinds of money are acceptable, others are not.

Legal tender status has become especially fuzzy recently with the advent of the **legal tender bullion coin**. These are coins produced under authority of a government and intended to be purchased at their intrinsic metal value for investment purposes. Many, however, have a face value well below their actual metal value, entirely opposite of debased coinage. Where a Washington quarter may have 3 cents worth of metal but a face value of 25 cents, an American Eagle gold bullion coin has $350 worth of

INVESTORS USE the face value of legal tender bullion coins as a hedge; if the price of the precious metal drops dramatically, the coin would still be worth its face value.

metal but only $50 face value. Of course, no one actually expects bullion coins to circulate at their face values, but their legal tender status means they *could*.

The problem becomes even fuzzier with Proof legal tender bullion coins. These are coins with a face value, but not intended either for circulation or for investment, but rather for collectors.

Also, commemorative coins are given face values and legal tender status, even though they are not intended for use as money, but as collectibles.

It seems that collectors of commemorative coins and investors in bullion coins like the assurances of legal tender status. Legal tender coins are viewed as "better" or more legitimate than non-legal tender coins or medals.

Coinage in America

The history of American coinage predates Independence, going back to the mid 1600s and the production of the Massachusetts silver New England, Willow, Oak and Pine Tree coins. The Colonial coins of Massachusetts and privately issued copper tokens were joined in circulation by a bewildering mass of foreign gold, silver and copper pieces, notably Spain's silver reales (pronounced "ree-AH-les").

The popular Spanish silver **8 reales**, the "piece of eight," was the model for the U.S. dollar. A real was referred to as a **"bit,"** or 12-1/2 cents — thus giving rise to the present-day cheer "two bits, four bits, six bits, a dollar . . ."

The various states — most notably New Jersey, Massachusetts and Connecticut — issued copper coins in quantity after Independence. (Vermont issued its coinage as an independent republic before it became a state.)

In 1787, Congress authorized the first official U.S. coinage, the copper **Fugio cents**. These privately-struck pieces are named for their design of a sundial with Latin motto meaning "I Fly," urging thrifty use of time. Some numismatists credit Benjamin Franklin with at least the idea for the Fugio cent design.

The new Philadelphia Mint ceremonially struck its first silver

THE MASSACHUSETTS BAY COLONY over a 30-year period in the 17th century produced a number of coins of varying design and denomination dated 1652, a year in which there was no king.

Though privately struck, the Fugio cents of 1787 are considered the first coins of the new United States government. The 13 linked rings on the reverse represent the original 13 states.

coin, the **half disme** (pronounced "deem"), in 1792. Coinage for general circulation began the next year with copper half cents and large cents, which continued until 1857.

A variety of precious and non-precious metals have been used in minting U.S. coins since circulating coinage began. Silver was used in circulating coinage until 1965 when **clad** coins, those made by bonding one metal to another, were introduced.

Gold coins were issued until 1933, when the financial crisis of the Great Depression resulted in all gold coinage being stopped by presidential order.

Silver and gold are now used by the United States Mint only for minting commemorative coins and legal tender bullion coins.

Manufacturing coins

The first coins were crudely-struck lumps of hot metal, usually off-center and often split. A lump of metal would be placed onto an anvil and struck with a hammer. If dies were used, the designs of the dies would be transferred to the coin. Because of the irregularity of the hand-hammering process, most early coins are off center, and many are split around the outside. They don't have well-defined edges that we would recognize as part of modern coinage.

Some early coins were cast in molds. A form is constructed and hot metal poured in. When the

Striking by hand often resulted in off-center and imperfectly shaped coins.

mold is broken open, coins are made. Many artists use variations of this process to create art medals today.

The **screw press** improved the consistency of coin production. With a screw press, a planchet is placed onto the lower die (still technically called the **"anvil die**," from the days of hammered coinage), and a weighted bar is turned, causing a screw to drive the **"hammer die"** into the coin metal. A hand-operated screw press requires a person to set the planchets and remove the struck coins, and one or two people to turn the screw. Still, it dramatically increased production over the hand-hammered method.

With the Industrial Revolution came powered presses. Steam power eventually replaced man- or horse-power. Coin production today, while much, much faster

This hand-operated screw press is on display at the Philadelphia Mint.

with modern hydraulics and electronic controls, nevertheless bears amazing similarity to early machine production.

Modern U.S. coins are produced in factories, called Mints, owned and operated by the federal government. Mints are located in Philadelphia, Pa.; Denver, Colo.; San Francisco, Calif.; and West Point, N.Y.

Smaller nations may employ a government Mint or private mint in another country to produce their coins.

There are many methods of producing coins in use around the world. But there are some general similarities of coin production. For our purposes, we will use the methods of the United States Mint as our example.

Coins begin as metallic ores, which are **assayed** (checked for the content of a specific metal or metals), refined, melted and formed into huge slabs of coinage alloy (mixture of more than one metal). The slabs are then passed through a series of rolling mills and are rolled flat to a specified thickness, at which point they

STEAM POWER was installed at the Philadelphia Mint in 1816, but the first steam-powered coining presses were not introduced until 1836.

are referred to as "**strip**."

Dime, quarter dollar and half dollar strip requires another step in which outer layers of copper-nickel are bonded to an inner core of pure copper. The coinage strip is trimmed and cleaned, then shipped to the Mint or to a private contractor for the production of planchets, also known as blanks.

To produce **planchets**, coinage strip is fed into heavy-duty punching machinery, which consists of a bank of metal punches and a lower steel bedplate full of holes aligned with the punches. The metal punches ram through the strip, punching out planchets on each downward cycle. Planchets are slightly larger than finished coins, and have rough edges,

Planchets are punched from strip.

or burrs, because of the shearing action of the punches. These rough edges are smoothed down during succeeding preparation steps.

Since 1982, U.S. cent planchets have required another production step because the planchet consists chiefly of zinc instead of copper. The zinc-alloy planchets are given a thin plating of pure copper to resemble pre-1982 brass cents.

The planchets are passed over sorting screens, called **riddlers**, designed to eliminate any undersized, non-round or otherwise defective blanks from getting into the coinage presses. The rejected planchets are melted for reuse.

During the finish rolling and blanking press operations, the planchets have been hardened and

Seen from above, cent planchets are sorted by screens.

must now be softened. To accomplish this, the sorted planchets are sent to an annealing furnace. During this **annealing**, or softening process, the planchets are passed through a cylinder with spiral grooves in its walls. The planchets are forced from one end of the cylinder to the other by the spirals as the cylinder turns. As the planchets travel through the cylinder, they are heated to approximately 1400 degrees Fahrenheit, changing their crystal structure to a softer state. By placing the softened planchets immediately into a water-quench bath, the planchets can be "frozen" into that state. This softening process reduces the striking pressure necessary to produce well-struck coins, thereby prolonging the life of the coining dies.

The heat of the annealing furnace discolors the planchets, which are chemically cleaned and dried by hot air. After being cleaned and dried, the planchets go

The upsetting mill forms a rim on planchets.

through the **upsetting mill** — a rotating grooved wheel inside a fixed grooved "shoe" which places a raised rim on each planchet. The distance between the grooves in the wheel and the grooves in the shoe lessens as the planchet travels along the grooved path, squeezing the planchet and slightly reducing its diameter and creating a raised **rim**.

The rim readies the striking of the coin by sizing and shaping the planchet for better feed into the press, and the process hardens the edge to prevent metal from escaping between the parts of the coining press.

To become a coin, each planchet is struck between a pair of **dies**, or hardened metal punches, bearing the same image that will appear on the coin, only reversed and incused (recessed). The design on each die is a mirror-image of what will appear on the coin.

Actually, the creation of a new coin begins long before the steps outlined above. Once a coin design has been approved it is sculptured in modeling wax three to twelve times the intended size

CIRCULATING COINS are usually struck only once, but some Proof coins and bullion coins are struck two or three times to sharpen the design details.

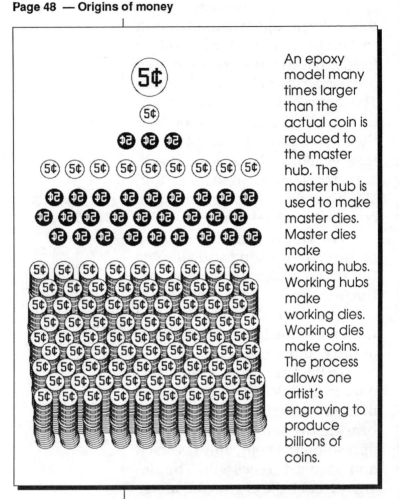

An epoxy model many times larger than the actual coin is reduced to the master hub. The master hub is used to make master dies. Master dies make working hubs. Working hubs make working dies. Working dies make coins. The process allows one artist's engraving to produce billions of coins.

of the coin, and negative and positive plasticene (synthetic modeling clay) models are made from the sculpture.

At each step, details are retouched to preserve the integrity of the design. The positive-image epoxy model is placed on a reduction engraving machine, which cuts the design into a piece of steel, creating a positive **master hub** the same size as the finished coin.

The master hub is heat-treated to harden it, and then used to create a number of **master dies**. The images on the master dies are backwards and incused — they look like inside-out coins. From these master dies, many **working hubs** are produced using the same process, and from each working hub are produced many **working dies**. The working dies are the actual dies used to strike coins.

Die pairs, or a matched obverse and reverse, are set into the **coining presses**. Some coining presses use just one die pair. These presses produce one coin at a time. They can run at very high speeds, or at slow speeds and at high pressures for producing collector coins.

Some presses used by the United States Mint have been

COIN ENGRAVERS once cut their designs directly into the dies, resulting in many small variations that are now collected by specialists.

Two Lincoln cent obverse dies are set together, enabling the press to strike more than one coin in each cycle.

modified to use more than one set of dies at a time. These presses can be set for two or four pairs of dies, and each cycle of the press produces two or four coins. These presses run at moderate speeds. They are used to strike circulating coinage, and the multiple dies are a means of increasing their output.

With each die pair is a **collar**. The collar is a circular piece of steel which forms the wall of a coining chamber, preventing the metal of the coin from spreading out beyond the confines of the dies when it is struck. The collar is sometimes referred to as the third die, because it can impress an image onto a coin's edge. The **reeding** on the half dollars, quarter dollars and dimes of the United

States are created with the collar. Similarly, the smooth edges of the cent and 5-cent piece are created by the collar.

More complex edge designs, such as lettering, generally require a separate process, either before or after the coin is struck. Because the metal of the coin expands into the recesses of the collar when the coin is struck, the collar's design must allow the coin to be ejected without interference.

To better understand this, find a coin with a reeded edge, and place it on the table with the obverse up. Remembering that a die is a reverse image of a coin, and that a collar with a

Among the many edge designs are plain, reeded, lettered and combination.

design can be considered a die, try to picture what happens when the coin is struck. The metal expands to fill the recesses in the collar. This expansion forms the raised ridges that we call reeding. Because the ridges are perfectly straight up and down, the coin can pop up out of the collar without interference.

Now, if there were letters cut into the collar, when the metal expanded into the recesses, the collar could not let go of the coin. Either the metal from the coin would be stuck in the collar, or the collar would be stuck in the surrounding coin metal. Therefore, irregular designs must be placed on the coin's edge in a separate step. This is done much like the upsetting mill process above, where the coins are rolled through a machine to impress the design.

Lettering is placed on some coins' edges in a process separate from striking.

Some complex edge designs were attempted in the early days of U.S. coinage. These grew out of the attempt to prevent shaving precious metal from the edges of coins, thereby cheating on a coin's value. Some experiments were made with spring-loaded segmented collars that opened and closed as the dies came together, but the difficulties made them impractical for large-scale use.

Many nations issue coins of odd shapes. These can range from triangular to square to many-sided to scalloped (a "frilly" shape). There is at least one practical reason: Irregular shapes help people identify denominations. In countries where illiteracy is high, odd-shaped coins are more common. Collectors enjoy these irregular pieces because they are exotic. Canada even employs non-round coins from time to time. The Loon dollar, for in-

Coins can be made in a variety of shapes.

Error coins are not only interesting, but sometimes reveal information about the manufacturing process.

stance, has a rounded, 11-sided shape.

While a coining press is in operation, the press operator inspects finished coins under magnification, looking primarily for defects caused by the dies. Improperly-shaped coins are kept out of circulation by a riddler, which sifts out defective coins.

Like any factory, the Mint makes mistakes, and sometimes these error coins escape into collector's hands. Errors are rare, but can be caused by broken or worn dies, by loose collars, or by more than one coin being fed between the dies at the time of striking. In some cases, a planchet is fed into the wrong press and struck with the design of another denomination coin. The number of error coins produced is small relative to the number of coins minted in any particular denomination. The number of error coins that make their way out of the Mint and into the hands of collectors is even smaller.

Rarity, though, does not necessarily mean great worth. Some error coins — even unique pieces — can be purchased for a few dollars. The values of error coins depend on the same factors as those for normal coins; supply, demand, and level of preservation.

How paper money is made

Modern U.S. paper money is printed at the Bureau of Engraving and Printing in Washington, D.C. Paper money is printed in sheets of 32 Federal Reserve notes using a three-stage intaglio process. Intaglio is from Italian, meaning "to cut in."

Intaglio printing involves the engraving of steel plates. Each design element is engraved sepa-

BEWARE OF an error that appears to be struck on a larger planchet than intended, such as a cent on a 5-cent planchet; larger-than-normal planchets will not fit into the collar to be properly struck.

rately by hand. Because the lines carved into the steel will eventually hold the ink to be printed on the paper, the engraver must do all of his work in mirror image. The elements, such as the portrait, framing, vignettes (pictures) and large numbers, are then combined to produce a master plate. The artistry of several engravers may be used on one note design.

The master plate is used to produce working plates, and the working plates are used to print the notes.

Because the plates are engraved, the presses do not merely lay down a design of ink on the paper. Instead, the paper is forced into the ink-filled lines of the plate, leaving a raised line of ink on the paper. By gently sliding

An engraver works his design — in reverse —directly into a steel plate.

Federal Reserve notes are printed in 32-note sheets, which are cut into 16-note sheets before being overprinted with serial numbers and seals.

the tips of your fingers over the surface of a new Federal Reserve note, you can feel those raised lines.

The green "backs" are printed first, followed by the black note "faces." Sheets are then cut in half and the 16-note half sheets receive the black and green **overprinting** which produces the Treasury and Federal Reserve Bank seals, index numbers and serial numbers, prior to being cut into individual notes.

The intricate manufacturing processes are security measures. The more complex a note is, the harder it is to counterfeit. Future notes of the United States may use such devices as security

Paper money of other countries can be fascinating. The white circle on the back contains a tiger watermark.

threads, which are plastic or metallic threads embedded in the paper during the paper manufacturing process. These will be visible when holding a note up to the light. Federal Reserve notes may also use micro-printing, which is extremely fine lettering noticeable only under magnification.

Security is already responsible for much of the way paper money looks and feels. The paper is a special blend of cotton, linen and other fibers. Tiny blue and red fibers are embedded in the paper (look closely, have you ever noticed these before?). The intaglio printing method itself, by being intricate and exacting work, is a security measure.

The paper money of other countries can be a colorful and fascinating collecting area. Foreign notes frequently use **watermarks**, which are designs built into the paper by varying the thickness during the paper manufacturing process. These can be seen when the note is held up to the light. Certain notes of Australia are experiments with plastic and **holograms**, which are three-dimensional images.

IT IS ILLEGAL for a private citizen to own the paper on which Federal Reserve notes are printed.

Knowing how a coin is minted or paper money is printed will help you better understand the origins and significance of money. Looking closely at your money will enable you to appreciate the artistry and craftsmanship that go into its manufacture. You will be able to compare the cultures of the world by comparing their money. And you will learn to distinguish manufacturing characteristics from circulation marks, which is very important when determining the value of your collectible items.

Grading

One
Two
Three
Four
Five
Six

Two factors affect the value of coins: their rarity, and their grade. Between two equally rare coins, the coin with the highest grade will generally be the more valuable. As prices for those often elusive perfect or near-perfect pieces continue to rise, the ability to accurately recognize a coin's grade becomes much more important. Paying for a piece that is overgraded can be expensive and discouraging.

The **grade**, or level of preservation, of a coin describes the amount of wear the coin has sustained since the moment it was manufactured. Coins range in grade from About Good, in which nearly all the designs on

COINS BEGIN TO WEAR as soon as they are struck, when they are ejected from the press into a bin with other new coins.

the obverse and reverse of the coin are heavily worn or missing, to **Mint State**, or **Uncirculated**, in which the coin is at or near the same level of preservation as when it was minted. Between About Good and Mint State are several additional grades — Good, Fine, Very Fine, Extremely Fine and About Uncirculated — which represent increasing levels of preservation. In addition to these grades, various grades may be further subdivided into grades indicated by numbers.

Grading becomes especially important in the case of Mint State coins. There are as many as 11 grades in Mint State. The scale runs from the lowest Mint State grade, MS-60, up to the MS-70 grade, the grade assigned perfectly flawless pieces. In some cases, grades are split. A grade of MS-60/63, for instance, refers to a Mint State coin with 60 referring to the level of preservation on the obverse side and 63 referring to the level of preservation on the reverse side.

The difference in worth between upper Mint State coins can be thousands of dollars, so it pays to know a coin's condition. For example, in the *1989 Coin World Guide to U.S. Coins, Prices & Value Trends*, a 1932-D Washington quarter dollar, struck at the Denver Mint and graded MS-63, is valued at $685. A 1932-D Washington quarter dollar graded MS-65 is valued at $3,300.

Each coin denomination and year of issue has its own special manufacturing, or striking, characteristics which may affect its grade.

A number of factors are taken into consideration when looking at Mint State coins: contact marks, luster, strike, toning and color and, most important to the coin collector, eye appeal. Not everyone uses all the factors when they grade coins.

Contact marks, often referred to as "bag marks," are minor abrasions on an otherwise Uncirculated coin. After coins are manufactured at

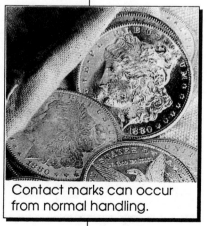

Contact marks can occur from normal handling.

the Mint, the coins are counted, sewn into cloth bags and then shipped to Federal Reserve Banks. The marks are caused by the coins hitting against each other in Mint-sewn bags, or by contact with other surfaces. The size, number and location of contact marks on a coin affect its grade.

Having a coin with a large number of contact marks will probably be unappealing to you. A small mark on a coin with a large diameter might go unnoticed unless placed under a magnifying lens. A large mark on a smaller-diameter coin will be more noticeable.

Another consideration is luster. **Luster** is the quality of a coin's surface, the result of light reflected from microscopic flow lines in the metal from which the coin is produced. When the pictures or designs are placed on the obverse and reverse in the

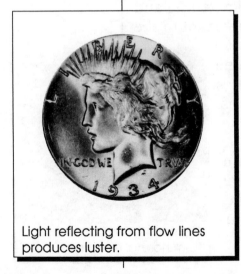

Light reflecting from flow lines produces luster.

manufacturing process, the metal in the planchet, or blank, flattens and spreads out. **Flow lines** result as the metal follows the outline of the picture being placed on the planchet to produce a coin. Coins with full luster generally have a bright surface, although toning, to be discussed shortly, can affect luster.

Any disturbance to the luster will affect the way light reflects off the surface. A coin whose luster has been disturbed may appear dull. Coins that are circulated do not exhibit luster because the microscopic flow lines have been worn away.

Luster on Mint State coins appears somewhat frosty in appearance as opposed to the mirror-like surface of Proof coins. Again, as discussed in the opening chapter, a Proof coin is one that is manufactured on specially-prepared metal planchets, or blanks, on special presses to receive the highest quality strike possible. Proof coins are produced especially for collectors.

A coin's **strike** refers to the sharpness of detail in the coin at

LUSTER CAN BE worn away in patches, remaining on protected areas of the coin's surface while disappearing from the high points.

the time it leaves the coin press. The strike occurs when the dies — hard metal punches that contain the obverse and reverse designs — press or strike the pictures into opposite sides of the planchets.

How much pressure is exerted at the time the dies strike the designs into the planchet, the condition of the planchet itself, the placement of the planchet to receive the impression of the dies, the amount of wear on the designs on the dies and the complexity of the designs can all affect the strike. A coin with a sharp strike contains clear details in the obverse and reverse designs and legends.

The sharpness of strike on a particular coin can affect the coin's grade, value or both, depending on who is inspecting the coin and what criteria they use.

Toning and color are also important in determining a coin's grade and value. A coin's original color may change over time in reaction to environmental factors. Copper coins, for instance, originally red in color, may turn brown

DIES, LIKE COINS, wear out with use; coins produced early in the die's life will usually show more detail than those produced toward the end.

or, depending on environmental influences, even green. Silver coins can change to any number of colors in the rainbow. It is not uncommon to see offered for sale silver half dimes, dimes, 20-cent pieces, quarter dollars, half dollars and dollars that have toned blue, pink, purple or shades of these and other colors.

Because gold is a more stable metal, it is rarely affected by environmental influences. Gold coins salvaged from treasure ships sunk hundreds of years ago in the ocean are still as bright and shiny as the day they were manufactured.

Rainbow toning is now considered desirable by many coin collectors and attractively, naturally-toned coins can be worth more and bring higher prices.

Unscrupulous individuals may artificially tone a coin using a variety of methods in an attempt to deceive the buyer into purchasing such a "beautiful-looking coin."

You may find it difficult at first to tell the difference between a coin that is naturally-toned and

OLD COPPER coins may develop a green color, called "verdigris," from the French for "green of the Greeks."

SOME PEOPLE have artificially toned coins using chlorine bleach and the heat of an oven.

one that has been artificially-toned. After you have looked over many coins, you will be able to notice the difference between the two. A coin that has been artificially toned will be worth less, because artificial toning is considered an alteration.

While looking for coins to add to your collection, you may find coins that are worn, yet appear to have a brilliant surface. In some cases, such coins have been **"dipped,"** treated with chemicals to remove what was once believed to be an unattractive surface for the coin. Dipping strips the outer surface off the coin and restores the brilliance but removes some of the metal in the process.

Despite the importance that accurate grading has for coin collecting, there is no one grading standard on which every collector or dealer can agree. The grading controversy lies between the grade assigned a particular coin by the dealer and the grade an individual might assign to the same coin. Ultimately, the value of a coin is determined by eye appeal. **Eye appeal** pertains to a coin's overall attractiveness, taking into consideration all the grading factors previously discussed. The eye appeal you believe a certain coin has will be as different from another coin collector's eye appeal as his fingerprints. When examining a coin, you must decide how attractive it is to your eye and whether you feel the coin is appealing enough, all things considered, to pay the price being asked to acquire the coin for your collection.

A FINGERPRINT on the surface of a coin detracts from its eye appeal, even though the coin may show no wear.

There are a number of numismatic publications that can assist you in learning about grading. The American Numismatic Association, an association of more than 30,000 collectors of coins and other numismatic material, published the *Official American Numismatic Association Grading Standards for United States Coins*, which contains photographs of the coins to help you.

Brown and Dunn's Guide to

the Grading of United States Coins uses drawings to illustrate the various grades. *Photograde* by James F. Ruddy makes use of actual photographs of the coins for each grade discussed.

Numismatic Certification Institute's *The NCI Grading Guide* by James L. Halperin contains photographs of coins and coin maps with colored areas to highlight areas on the coins where wear, contact marks and other disturbances can affect a coin's grade.

EXPERTS AGREE that the best way to learn grading is to examine a large number of coins.

If you're collecting U.S. coins, you should become familiar with at least one of the four grading guides mentioned, but should not ignore the advice of collector friends who have years of experience in grading coins.

Another aspect of grading that you should be aware of is the advent of **grading services** that will grade your coins for a fee.

The **International Numismatic Society Authentication Bureau** (INSAB) in Washington, D.C., began grading coins in 1976 and three years later the **American Numismatic Association Certification Service** (ANACS) began its grading service. ANACS and INSAB will grade your coin and provide a color photo containing the certified grade of the coin.

A number of privately-operated grading services have sprouted up over the years, most notably the **Professional Coin Grading Service** (PCGS) in Newport Beach, Calif., **Numismatic Guaranty Corporation of America** (NGC) in Parsippany, N.J., and the **Numismatic Certification Service** (NCI) in Dallas, Texas.

Encapsulated or "slabbed" coins were introduced to the coin collecting world by PCGS in February 1986 as a solution to the grading controversy. NGC and NCI also offer slabbed coins and ANACS and INSAB began offering the service in 1989. A slabbed coin is one that has been sent to a grading service, examined by one or more numismatists, assigned a grade and then placed in a sealed, plastic holder or "slab"

SOME SLABS use holograms as security devices against tampering or counterfeiting.

The "slab" is a relatively recent development.

that also contains a slip of paper identifying the type of coin and grade.

The slab also contains numbers used to identify a specific coin and can be used to track a coin if it changes hands. Slabbed coins are usually Mint State or Proof coins.

Slabs are sometimes traded by dealers and investors "sight-unseen"; that is, they are bought and sold without the buyer ever having to see the coin, assured that the grade assigned the coin truly represents its level of preservation. The price paid for a coin graded and then placed into a plastic slab is usually higher than that for the same coin in the "raw" stage, outside a holder.

Unlike the individual who buys high-grade or rare coins strictly as an investment, coin collectors often prefer "raw" coins because in that state the coin's edge, is clearly visible and can be inspected for impairments the collector feels may lower the value of a coin.

Be aware that the grade assigned to a coin by one service may not be the same grade assigned by another service inspecting the same coin. Grading guidelines may differ from grading service to grading service, or different services may interpret the same guidelines more conservatively or more loosely,

In addition to grading coins, services such as ANACS and INSAB will, again for a fee, authenticate coins. Discovering that a coin you just purchased is a complete fake or is a genuine coin altered to resemble a more valuable coin is enough to make anyone want to give up coin collecting and look for another hobby. Unfortunately, it is likely counterfeit and altered coins will continue to be found in the numismatic market in the future.

A **counterfeit** coin is a total

FEW COUNTERFEITS are good enough to fool the experts; they are usually intended to mislead the inexperienced or unwary.

fake, produced outside the government Mint which issued the real coin.

An **altered** coin is a genuine coin of lower value, which is then altered — through the removal or addition of a Mint mark, or the alteration of a date, for example — to resemble a rarer and thus more expensive coin.

For instance, someone might take a genuine 1922-D Lincoln cent in Good condition and remove the "D" Mint mark identifying the piece as having been manufactured at the Denver Mint. The genuine 1922-D cent with the Mint mark is worth $3.35 in Good condition. The genuine 1922 "Plain" cent, minus the Mint mark, is worth $130.

THE HOBBY PROTECTION ACT requires reproductions or imitations of coins and other numismatic items to be permanently marked with the word "COPY."

A related bogus numismatic item, the **replica**, is generally a cast copy of some non-U.S. Mint coin or token or paper copy of a non-federal note produced as a souvenir. Both items turn up with regularity in dealers' junk boxes.

A beginning collector should not let the possibility of acquiring a counterfeit or an altered coin prevent him from enjoying coin collecting as it was meant to be enjoyed. Professional coin dealers can help you acquire experience in detecting counterfeits. Reputable dealers have developed expertise through years of working with thousands of coins. A dealer who fails to develop a working

This dime has been made to appear as a valuable error by impressing the reverse of a cent into clear glue.

knowledge of coin authentication will drive himself out of business by his own ignorance. Deal only with reputable, knowledgeable dealers. Pass up opportunities that seem to good to be true. They probably are.

If you have doubts about the authenticity of a particular coin, send it to one of the major authentication services, such as the American Numismatic Association Certification Service (818 North Cascade Ave., Colorado Springs, Colo. 80901; telephone (719) 632-2646); or International

Numismatic Society Authentication Bureau (Box 66555, Washington, D.C. 20035; telephone (202) 223-4496).

Many dealers are willing to send coins to such services, with instructions that the service make out certificates of authenticity and send them, along with the coins, directly to the collector if the coin is judged genuine. If the service decides the coin is not genuine, it is returned to the dealer and the collector's money is refunded.

COLLECTORS OF ERROR coins or notes must be especially aware of authenticity.

Some specialty coin collecting clubs whose members have similar collecting interests — such as those focusing on Civil War tokens, early American Colonial coins, error and variety coins — often offer authentication services free to members only. Check with the organization or firm as to the services provided and specific charges.

Books that may help you in learning about counterfeits and altered coins and paper money are Don Taxay's *Counterfeits, Misstruck and Unofficial U.S. Coins*, Bert Harshe's *How to Detect Altered & Counterfeit Coins and*

Paper Money, and *The Official Guide to Detecting Altered & Counterfeit U.S. Coins & Currency* by Mark Hudgeons.

In addition to these sources of information, serious collectors may at some point wish to consider attending a training seminar on counterfeit detection and grading. Each summer the ANA provides a very popular seminar on this subject.

You should get what you pay for. Being aware of what you are buying and its level of preservation can save you a lot of money and anguish. If you are new to coin collecting, or if you're on a limited budget, you may want to start your collection with coins in lower grades, replacing them with coins in higher grades as you gain expertise.

Finally, as you develop your collection, learn all you can about the minting process. An educated collector is the numismatic counterfeiter's worst enemy. As in any other endeavor, experience is a valuable teacher.

KNOWLEDGE IS your best protection against overgraded or phony coins.

Guide to grading terms

The following guides are not presented as grading standards, but as introductions to the terminology of grading and its usage.

A few words regarding grading usage. When two grades are linked together by a slash — as in Mint State 65/63 — it means that the coin has two grades; the first grade represents the obverse and the second, the reverse. When two grades are linked by a hyphen — as in Mint State 65-63 — it means that the grade for both sides is indeterminate and lies somewhere between the two grades given. Sometimes, a combination of both usages will appear, as in MS-60/60-63, meaning the obverse grades MS-60 and the reverse somewhere between MS-60 and MS-63.

Plus signs (+) are used by many to indicate a coin slightly better than the numerical grade indicated, but not as good as the next numerical grade. A coin graded MS-60+ is better than an MS-60 coin, but not as good as an MS-61 coin.

Many dealers and collectors

use adjectives instead of numerals, or combine adjectives and numerals when speaking about Mint State coins. A superb or superb gem coin is generally MS-67, and a gem coin is usually MS-65. Some dealers use choice to describe an MS-63 coin, and others use choice for an MS-65 coin. Mint State 60 coins are generally referred to as Uncirculated or Brilliant Uncirculated; sometimes an MS-60 coin is called typical Uncirculated. Collectors should determine what adjectival "system" the dealer uses when no numerals are present because of the disagreement over what the adjectives represent numerically.

Buyers should remember that different dealers and different collectors or investors use different grading systems. Even though various grading services use an 11-point Mint State system, this does not necessarily mean they use the same criteria for assigning grades. In fact, there is no universally-accepted standard for determining grades for U.S. coins.

Proof: Traditionally, Proof describes a method of manufacture only, and not a grade. However, since numerals are often assigned to Proof coins, there are different qualities of Proof coins; in effect, different grades. A circulated Proof is often called an "impaired Proof." Proof is rarely abbreviated.

Mint State and Uncirculated: The two terms are interchangeable and describe a coin which has no wear. To qualify as Mint State, a coin may not have any level of wear. Even the slightest amount of wear will drop the coin into the About Uncirculated level. (Also, coins described by some dealers as "Borderline Uncirculated" have wear and are actually About Uncirculated.) Mint State is most often used with numerals. The numerical Mint State system so widely used in the current rare coin market is based on a system created by Dr. William H.

Sheldon for the U.S. large cents of 1793-1814. It has since spread to U.S. coins in general. Uncirculated is usually abbreviated as Unc.; it often appears as Brilliant Uncirculated, abbreviated as BU. Sometimes used with numerals, generally as Unc. 60, and so on.

About Uncirculated: This is a coin with only the barest traces of wear on the highest points of the design. It is abbreviated AU and often appears with numerals as AU-50, AU-55 and AU-58. The term has gained acceptance despite seeming inconsistency. Some people in the hobby still say that no coin can be About Uncirculated — it is either Uncirculated or it's not. Some use Almost Uncirculated, although all major U.S. grading guides use "About."

Extremely Fine: Light overall wear on highest points, but with all design elements sharp and clear. It is abbreviated by most hobbyists as EF, although a few use XF. It appears as EF-40 and EF-45.

Very Fine: The coin has light to moderate even wear on surface and high points of design. Abbreviated VF, it appears with numerals as VF-20 and VF-30. The abbreviations VF-25 and VF-35 are infrequently used.

Fine: The wear is considerable although the entire design is still strong and visible. It is abbreviated as F-12.

Very Good: The design and surface are well worn, main features are clear but flat. Abbreviated as VG, it is used with numeral as VG-8 and VG-10.

Good: Design and surface are heavily worn, with some details weak and many details flat. It is abbreviated only when used with numeral, G-4; G-6 is infrequently used. Ironically, a coin in Good condition is not a "good" coin to collect; a Good coin is generally the lowest collectible grade.

About Good: The design is heavily worn with surface fading into rim, many details weak or missing. Abbreviated as AG, it is used with a numeral as AG-3. Few coins are collectible in About Good condition. Dealers also use the terms Fair and Fair 3 to describe a coin in this state of preservation.

Paper money terms:

New and **Uncirculated** — Terms are interchangeable, and often preceded by "Crisp." A new note cannot show any folds, creases or tears, but may show bank teller handling, including pinholes. Notes that have the image well-centered on each side and even margins bring a premium over more typical notes. Crisp Uncirculated is abbreviated CU.

Extremely Fine — Must retain crispness, but may have a light center fold or light corner fold, no major tears or stains. Abbreviated EF or sometimes XF.

Very Fine — Some crispness must remain, two to four folds or corner creases, but no tears. Has seen moderate circulation, but still attractive to the eye and to the touch. Several small stains or one larger stain are permitted, but should not detract from the general appearance of the note. Abbreviated VF.

Fine — Horizontal and vertical folds and creases are well-defined. Most of the crispness is gone, some limpness may be noticeable. Seen considerable circulation and may have one or two minor tears. It may have some larger, more noticeable stains detracting from the note's general appearance. Generally not abbreviated.

Very Good — Well-worn, with considerable folding and limpness. Note may be dirty, but not filthy. The print may have worn away along the heavy creases.

Good — Note is ragged and dirty, and may have holes, large tears, missing corners and considerable wear and damage.

Other common grading terms:

Fleur de Coin — Often used for foreign coins, it is basically the same as Uncirculated.

Mediocre — For ancient coins, the coin is identifiable, with some design still recognizable.

Poor — For ancient coins, heavily damaged or corroded, perhaps not even identifiable.

Storing and handling

Good judgment alone dictates that coins should not be abused, mishandled or stored loosely with other coins in a way that can cause dents, nicks or scratches.

How you pick up your coins is important. Handle your coins as little as possible, but when you must handle them, never pick them up with your fingers touching the obverse or reverse sides of the coin. Dirt and other contaminants on your hands, not to mention the natural oils of your skin, can react with the surface metal of the coin and cause irreversible damage. The only proper way to handle a coin is by placing the coin between the thumb and forefinger, holding the edge of the

Learn to handle your coins without risking damage to them.

coin and rotating it between those fingers to inspect its various details. You may even want to purchase an inexpensive pair of cotton gloves to avoid transferring any contaminants from your hands to your coins. Grading services always use such precautions when handling customers' coins.

Don't breathe directly on your coins. This may sound humorous to the beginning collector, but advanced hobbyists know that warm, moist breath can affect the surfaces of coins, especially the delicate surfaces of Proof coins.

When examining your coins, use a velvet or velvet-like padded mat, similar to those you might see in a jeweler's display case. Place the mat flat on a table to catch any coin that might happen to fall out of its holder while you are handling it. Make sure the pad is thick enough to completely cushion a coin's unanticipated fall. Gold coins in particular are very soft, and dropping them on a hard surface can result in permanent damage that detracts from their beauty and value. This extra care can help you avoid adding dents, scratches and other unwanted blemishes to your coins.

Many collectors and investors are tempted to clean their coins. Each year, countless numbers of coins are ruined forever by misguided attempts at cleaning. Coins that have been handled improperly or have suffered corrosion or other reactions to the environment can be cleaned, but in many cases this is a job for experts. Collectors never want coins in their collection that show even the slightest hint of having been cleaned.

Ideally, coins should look as if they have been preserved in their natural state. When coins are originally new and bright, you should of course attempt to keep

THE ACT OF using a wire brush to "shine up" a coin is called "whizzing."

GOLD IS VERY RESISTANT to tarnish, but smokers beware! Tobacco can stain gold.

them at that level of preservation. But keep in mind that circulated coins which have their original Mint sheen worn away can never have this luster restored. No amount of polishing or cleaning will make a new coin out of one that has been in circulation, and stripping the outside film (called the **patina**, in the case of copper or silver coins) that naturally develops on a coin after a number of years will only leave the coin's surface exposed to further and possibly more serious damage.

Keep in mind, too, that natural toning is considered an attractive feature to many collectors — so much so that some unscrupulous individuals attempt to create toning artificially. In any case, most collectors prefer coins showing the darkening of age or natural toning over coins that have been stripped of these features by improper cleaning. Coins that have been naturally toned should be left alone.

Coins that have been subjected to chemical cleaners are said to have been **"dipped."** Dipping strips off surface metal from a coin and leaves the coin with a shiny but unnatural finish. Collectors avoid dipped coins, because there is no way of knowing how many times a coin has been dipped before it has been offered for sale.

Does all this mean you yourself should never under any circumstances attempt to clean coins that have accumulated dirt, been smudged, or which are tarnished? Not at all — but you should exercise caution, especially in the case of rare or valuable coins. Loose dirt can generally be removed by carefully washing coins with a good-quality soap, after which they should be patted dry with a soft tissue. Coins should never be brushed or rubbed with any abrasive or rough object, which can cause the removal of surface metal and lessen the value of the coin.

WHILE COINS are quite durable for circulation, their surfaces are delicate.

There are a number of commercial coin cleansers available. If you wish to use them, experiment first on coins of no special value, and then use them on valuable coins only after you have gained experience and if, in the

AIR POLLUTION is particularly hard on silver coins, which react with sulfur and nitrate compounds.

opinion of an expert, such cleaning would be to your advantage.

Perhaps the best advice that can be given with regard to cleaning coins is to avoid the necessity for it. In addition to handling coins properly, that means storing them to prevent, or at least greatly slow down, the natural processes of oxidation and surface decay that result from exposure to the environment.

A wide spectrum of storage devices is available. At one end of the spectrum are devices designed for easy viewing and access or short-term storage; at the other end of the spectrum are long-term storage devices designed to preserve coins in a natural condition indefinitely.

Chances are, the coin you purchased from the dealer at your local coin shop or at a coin show came in a holder that is not suitable for long-term storage. Many of the less-expensive coins in a dealer's inventory are kept in thin plastic pockets slipped inside small paper envelopes. Another popular device for storing individual coins in dealers' inventories consists of small folded cardboard holders with clear plastic windows in the middle so you can see the obverse and reverse of the coin. These holders can be stapled shut on all four sides, sealing the coin between the sides of the holder. The windows are of varying sizes to accommodate the various denominations of coins to be stored. Information about the coins can be written on the outside.

Some of these paper holders are undesirable because they contain

There are many types of holders available to the collector.

sulfur in sufficient quantity to react with the surface metal on your coin, reducing its level of preservation and value.

A similar problem exists in the case of some plastic coin **"flips."** Flips come in different sizes to hold different coin denominations. Each flip has two sides, which fold over, and each side has a pocket. One pocket holds the coin, the other a paper insert that can be written on to

HEAT AND SUNLIGHT can speed up chemical reactions and damage your collectibles.

indicate pertinent information about the coin. Flips are convenient short-term storage devices, frequently used by dealers at coin conventions or shows because they are soft and pliable and allow all three sides of the coin to be easily viewed. Some flips, though, contain **polyvinylchloride**, otherwise known as **"PVC."** It wasn't until several years after the introduction of flips containing PVC that dealers and collectors began noticing a greenish or blue slime or stain on many of their coins.

The discoloration was found to be permanent in many instances. In addition, removing the coins from these holders after years of storage sometimes resulted in part of the holder sticking to the surface of the coin, causing further damage. It was found that chemicals in the PVC were bleeding out of the film onto the coins. Many collectors like to remove the coin from the PVC flip and place it into another flip, one containing no PVC or other chemical that will react with the metal in the coin and cause damage.

Some coin folders that house

coins like a fold-out book, as well as coin tubes to store rolls of coins, also contain PVC. Other holders for long-term storage are made of acrylic or plastic, especially those seen on the bourse floor housing earlier dated Uncirculated and Proof sets. The 2-by-2-inch polystyrene holders are of convenient storage size, and are suitable for display purposes in coin exhibits. Their special construction offers nearly complete protection for an indefinite period of time.

Slabs, those specially-sealed plastic holders housing mostly Uncirculated and Proof coins graded by grading services, are also considered long-term storage holders. Still another popular holder is made of triacetate with two circular halves that snap together with the coin snug in between. There are other similar snap-together plastic holders in varying shapes and sizes.

Clear plastic sandwich-type holders are also popular. Available in a variety of shapes and sizes to accommodate individual coins or sets, these devices are

BECAUSE CONTAMINANTS may be embedded in the coin's metal, even airtight seals are no guarantee against corrosion.

held together with plastic screws around the perimeter, securing the two halves of the holder and the center insert.

The value and level of preservation of the coin or coins you have purchased will have a lot to do with making the decision about the means of storage you want to follow. Circulated coins are not at risk to the same degree as Uncirculated or Proof coins. Keep in mind, though that whatever kind of coins you collect, improper storage can cost you your collection.

EVEN PROOF COINS sealed in holders by the Mint have already been exposed to potentially damaging contaminants.

Remember, too, that no matter how well you preserve your coins, they will be subject to oxidation and tarnish when exposed to normal environmental conditions. Collectors living in areas with high levels of air pollution or excessive humidity must take extra precautions in caring for their collections. In coastal areas, salt air can be particularly corrosive. The only sure way to preserve a coin in its natural condition is to keep it embedded in some kind of plastic, or sealed in a completely air-tight container.

The drawback to this kind of storage is in not being able to get to the coin when you want to examine or display it.

You want to use a holder that will best preserve each coin in your collection while allowing easy access, and you don't want to have to keep switching your coins from holder to holder. Excessive handling of your coins can cause just as much damage as putting the coins in the wrong kind of holder. Any of the 2-by-2-inch or similar size coin holders for individual coins can be stored in cardboard or plastic slide trays or storage boxes. Boxes and trays come in single- and double-row sizes and allow storage of a large number of individual coins. The boxes and trays also allow you to transport a large number of coins conveniently. Care should be taken to select a type of box or tray that is as airtight as possible.

In addition to the storage methods already discussed, pressed board coin folders and albums are popular with beginning collectors for housing circu-

THE KIND OF HOLDERS you decide upon will depend on whether you frequently travel with your collection.

Many collectors got their start by filling a coin album.

lated coins in lower grades. These holders, which are manufactured by specific coin type, issue and denomination, allow you to press your coins in place in each of the openings of each page. The openings to accommodate each coin are arranged by date and Mint mark, and on some folders have the mintage of that particular issue printed below the opening. While this kind of holder is very popular among beginners, it only allows you to see one side of the coin, either obverse or reverse, depending on which side is facing out.

Be careful about storing coins in folders or albums that have see-through slides or windows. Moving these slides or windows back and forth can, over time, cause wear marks on the high points on the surfaces of your coins. You can store rolls of coins of plastic coin tubes sealed with tape to prevent the tops from accidentally falling off and spilling out the contents.

Collectors of paper money should exercise the same common-sense cautions that apply to coins. They must also take care not to fold, crease or tear the paper items, as all of these will reduce its value.

Also, collectible paper items that may be torn should never be taped, and marks should not be erased.

A few highly trained specialists have the know-how to neutralize acidic papers and clean valuable items. Attempting to do so without the proper training can permanently ruin your valuable collectible.

PAPER MONEY should not be stored in basements, or in any place where molds can develop.

Where you store your collection is as important as what you store your collection in. Avoid subjecting coins, paper money and other numismatic items to extremes of moisture, heat, or direct sunlight, as these can speed up the natural processes of decay or impairment. The goal of stor-

SOME MATERIALS used in handling and storing coins can be poisonous or flammable; follow directions carefully.

ing coins is to keep your coins in as secure an airtight environment as possible to protect them from contaminants that may be floating in the air. It is important you store your coins in a cool, dry place. Dampness and humidity can cause surface damage and corrosion to your coins. The kind and extent of damage depends on the severity of dampness and humidity and the coin's metal content. Storing silica gel along with the coins to remove moisture, especially if you live in a humid environment, may prove helpful. Many numismatic supply companies offer specially formulated moisture inhibitors that cost only a few dollars and are well worth the investment.

It is also recommended that you maintain a written record of your collection. The record should describe each item, where it was purchased, its condition at time of purchase, and the price. It is fine to keep this record with your collection, but you should also keep a copy in a safe place separate from the collection. That way, if your collection is stolen, you will have a complete record to supply to authorities, and for insurance purposes.

Finally, no matter how or where you store your coins, be sure to inspect them occasionally to see that no harmful tarnish has developed. It is an unusual collector who does not enjoy looking at his coin collection from time to time.

Coins are not as indestructible as most people think. They are delicate works of art that should be handled accordingly. The slightest mistake could prove very expensive. Knowing and practicing the basics of proper handling and storage is a big step toward assuring that your coins age the way they were meant to age.

RARE COINS should be preserved for the next generation of collectors.

Security should concern even the newest collector. Storing your collection at home is ideal if you want to have access to your coins at a moment's notice, but it may not always be safe. Since coins and paper money are currency, and usable as a medium of ex-

IT IS FUN TO DISPLAY items from your collection, but take care not to attract the attention of the wrong person.

change, they are attractive to thieves for their face value alone.

Some collectors keep their coins in a safe at home, or hide them so they have convenient access to their collection. As for hiding your coins, remember that you are an amateur while the person from whom you wish to hide them may be a professional. It is highly doubtful that you will fool him for long.

Security measures such as dead-bolt locks on doors, locks on windows, alarms and other means of protection for your collection should be considered as you would consider your home's protection without a coin collection. If you do leave your collection at home, remember that no technique is positive prevention against a professional thief. The history of thefts from major "secure" museum and private collections should be ample proof of this.

It is wise to be discreet about your home collection. Most of us enjoy sharing our hobby with others, making total discretion difficult. Still, there are a few common-sense steps you can take to address this problem. When buying or selling coins through the mail, for instance, it's smart not to advertise on the outside of an envelope that you are a coin collector. Some collectors request that dealers from whom they purchase coins not print the name of their business on their envelopes. Many collectors rent a post office box and have all correspondence dealing with coins sent to that address rather than to their home address.

If your coin collection contains coins of considerable worth, you may want to consider storing them in a safe-deposit box at your local bank. Selecting the right kind of safe-deposit room is important. A safe-deposit box room that is air-conditioned and climate-controlled is considered best. You may want to avoid one which has an ozone purification system. Such a system emits a germ-killing agent that will corrode certain kinds of coins very quickly. If you do decide to put your coins in a bank's safe-deposit box, read the rental agree-

IF YOU MAKE frequent visits to your safe-deposit box, vary your routine so as not to attract the attention of professional thieves.

ment carefully. The agreement spells out the terms and the liability on the bank's part should something happen to your collection.

Based on the value of your collection as it grows, you may decide that you should have a home safe in which to temporarily store those items on which you are working until you can return them to the bank.

Whether you keep your coins at home or at a bank, make it a point to check with your insurance agent about what type of coverage is needed to protect your collection. Keep a descriptive list of your coins, and photographs of the more valuable pieces, in a safe place away from where the coins are stored as an added protection in the event of theft or natural disaster.

As a collector, an investor, or both, it will do little good to use sound judgment in putting together a collection or portfolio only to see your efforts wiped out as the result of careless handling, improper storage, or theft.

Building a library

One
Two
Three
Four
Five
Six

Every coin collector and investor should have a numismatic library, whether it includes a few, carefully-chosen books or an extensive collection of volumes covering a variety of numismatic topics. A well-chosen numismatic library is necessary for the full enjoyment of coin collecting. You will find yourself turning often from your collection to your library as your thirst for numismatic knowledge grows.

Coins reflect man's history. Numismatic books record that history with a numismatic perspective. Your collecting interests help direct you to the right reference works. At the same time, reference works can help you decide what direction your collection will take.

A good place to start looking for reference works is in the classified advertisements printed weekly in *Coin World*. You will also find dealers offering the latest in numismatic books. Many of the dealers who advertise in the classifieds specialize in such books. Purchasing books through these ads can introduce you to book specialists. Book specialists not only offer books at competitive prices to fit the budgets of most collectors, but also offer, usually through mail-bid sale or auction, out-of-date reference books that often command high prices.

Other sources for numismatic books include your local coin dealer, newsstands and bookstores. Should the book you want not be in stock at any of these establishments, they may be able to order it for you from a book wholesaler, or directly from the publisher.

Coin shows are another source of reference materials. Coin dealers often bring books for sale

FINDING THE RIGHT reference book can be as challenging as finding the right coin.

with them to coin shows, and book specialists normally attend the larger coin conventions.

A valuable reference source that is often overlooked is the auction catalog. The larger numismatic auction houses devote a large amount of energy and resources to producing catalogs for auctions.

These auction catalogs are generally well-illustrated, often with full color pages as well as black and white. Professional numismatists describe the principal lots in great detail.

Subscribing to the catalogs of one or two auction houses is reasonable. You will find firms that tend to offer the type of material you are interested in. You can then use the catalogs as valuable references. By tracking the prices realized, which are generally available after the results of the auction are compiled, you

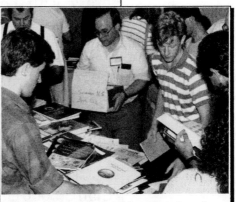

Collectors can find books about every numismatic subject.

have an accurate source for determining the value of certain types of material.

Visit your local library to see what kinds of numismatic books it has on its shelves. Major public libraries and libraries on college campuses usually have selections of numismatic books. You will find most librarians happy to accept suggestions and recommendations for books they may want to buy for their libraries.

SPECIALTY CLUBS often maintain their own reference libraries for use by members.

Being able to check out a numismatic book from your local library for a few weeks often can help you decide whether you want to purchase the book for your home library. Remember, too, that many local coin clubs have a library with books available for members to borrow.

One advantage of membership in the American Numismatic Association is that the ANA maintains the world's largest free, circulating numismatic library.

The ANA library has more than 35,000 circulating volumes. Most of these are available for only a few dollars each to cover postage and insurance both ways. Rarer reference works which are not available for loan can, in some instances, be used in the ANA library itself if you are fortunate enough to arrange a visit to ANA headquarters in Colorado Springs, Colo. Volumes available in the ANA Library cover all aspects of United States and world numismatics: coins, paper money, tokens, medals, orders and decorations, and stocks and bonds.

In addition to books, you will find one of the finest selections of auction catalogs in the world plus a wide range of numismatic periodicals, including nearly 30 years of *Coin World* on microfilm. The ANA Library catalog, covering several hundred pages, provides a complete listing of numismatic literature.

The books discussed below are used often by *Coin World* staff writers when researching information for articles. Some of the books are out of print, though

FOR A FEE the ANA library staff will do research on some topics.

available through numismatic book dealers. Other older volumes have been reprinted in modern editions.

For beginning collectors especially, these inexpensive reprints are recommended over the expensive original editions. Some of the original editions are hundreds of years old and collectors' items themselves.

U.S., general

The 320-page, pocket-sized *Coin World Guide to U.S. Coins, Prices & Value Trends*, introduced in 1989, presents for the first time in book form, price performance graphs tracking more than 16,576 United States coin values. Written by *Coin World* News Editor William T. Gibbs, with coin Trends values compiled by *Coin World* Trends Editor Keith M. Zaner, the book provides a straight-forward approach to collecting and investing in U.S. coins, containing essential information about rarity, grading, pricing, buying and selling coins, and the performance of individual coin issues in the numismatic market. Also included in the book is capsule information about coins series and types, along with actual-size photographs for you to quickly and easily identify U.S. coins. The book, to be published annually with updated information, comprises 14 chapters, including a glossary of numismatic terms; a unified history of U.S. coins, divided into sections covering denominations, specifications and designs; a brief history of the U.S. Mints, with information about locating Mint marks; grading; the cyclical nature of the coin market; mintage figures; error coins; "classic rarities," defined as those pieces with mysterious origins such as the 1804 dollar and 1913 Liberty Head 5 cents; and "necessity money," covering the pre-federal coinages, Hard Times and Civil War token issues, and pioneer gold coins.

Walter Breen's Complete Encyclopedia of U.S. and Colonial Coins, published in 1988 by Doubleday, fills 754 pages and is illustrated with more than 4,000 photographs. Considered the definitive U.S. numismatic reference book, Breen's book explores coin issues from Colonial pieces to modern U.S. commemoratives. The book describes in detail every major and minor U.S. coin, including the first brass Bermuda shillings issued in 1616 to such recent issues as the State of Liberty commemorative coins in 1986. According to Doubleday, the more than 7,800 entries in Breen's book represent more than four times as much information as can be found in any other book of its kind.

Other books to consider:

Annual Report of the Director of the Mint. United States Mint, Department of the Treasury, issued annually. A valuable source for numismatists, with mintage figures, photographs of new coins and medals, reports about new coinage programs, reports about technology changes at the Mint, charts about gold and silver deposits to the Mint and more. May be ordered from the United States Mint, Treasury Department, Washington, D.C. 20220.

Coin World Almanac. **Staff of *Coin World.*** Amos Press Inc., Sidney, Ohio 45365. 1987. One-volume general reference, includes chronologies of United States and world numismatics; history of precious metals; legal issues relating to coinage; other sections relating to collecting coins and paper money. Four earlier editions, dated 1976, 1977, 1978 and 1984.

The Coin Collector's Survival Manual. **Travers, Scott A.** Second edition, 1988, Prentice Hall Press, New York. First edition, 1984, Arco Publishing, Inc., New York. Includes ways of refining your method of looking at coins;

grading; grading services; telling Proof from prooflike; how to get the most out of price guides; guarantees and mail-order coin buying; the role of the coin convention; how to sell your coins; cleaning coins; how to choose the right coin holder; and safekeeping of your coins.

The Catalogue & Encyclopedia of U.S. Coins. Taxay, Don. Scott Publishing, New York, 1976. Includes patterns, rarity ratings for many pieces, pedigrees of rarer coins and all regular issues, commemoratives, Colonials, state issues and pioneer gold.

A Guide Book of United States Coins. Yeoman, R.S. Western Publishing Company, Racine, Wis., annually since 1947. Basic catalog listing of U.S. Colonial, state, Mint and commemorative coins, plus pioneer gold; the "Red Book."

A Handbook of United States Coins. Yeoman, R.S. Western Publishing Co., Racine, Wis., annually. Formerly hard-cover, now soft-cover, this guide is for the beginning collector of U.S. coins; the "Blue Book."

The History of United States Coinage as Illustrated by the Garrett Collection. **Bowers, Q. David.** Bowers and Ruddy Galleries, Inc., Los Angeles, Calif., 1979. Covers the history of U.S. coins and collecting, with numerous letters and other documents quoted extensively.

The Macmillan Encyclopedic Dictionary of Numismatics. **Doty, Richard G.** Macmillan Publishing Co., New York, 1982. Illustrated dictionary, plus bibliography.

Numismatic Art in America. **Vermeule, Cornelius.** Belknap Press of Harvard University Press, Cambridge, Mass., 1971. Examines the aesthetics of U.S. coinage, and traces development of engraving skills of U.S. engravers.

U.S. Mint and Coinage. **Taxay, Don.** Durst Numismatic Publications, New York, 1983 (reprint of 1966 book). Early history of U.S. Mint and minting processes in detail, plus history from mid-19th century to modern coinage.

Colonial, pioneer, patterns

California Pioneer Fractional Gold. **Breen, Walter, and Gillio, Ronald J.** Pacific Coast Auction Galleries Inc., Santa Barbara, Calif., 1983. Catalog listing of varieties of California fractional gold, including black-and-white photos of most coins.

The Early Coins of America. **Crosby, Sylvester S.** Quarterman Publications Inc., New York, 1983 (facsimile reprint of 1875 book). Covers all Colonial, Confederation and state issues, with extracts from authorizing legislation, plus plates.

Encyclopedia of United States and Colonial Proof Coins 1722-1977. **Breen, Walter.**

FCI Press, Inc., Albertson, N.Y., 1977. Historical information and pedigrees about U.S. Proofs, with sections covering branch Mint Proofs and fantasy and restrike pieces.

***Private Gold Coins and Patterns of the United States.* Kagin, Donald H.** Arco Publishing Inc., New York, 1981. History and catalog of pioneer gold, excluding fractional parts of a dollar.

***United States Pattern, Experimental and Trial Pieces.* Judd, J. Hewitt, and Kosoff, A.** Western Publishing Co. Inc., Racine, Wis., 1982. Covers all non-issued U.S. coin designs in catalog form, with illustrations, pedigrees, rarity ratings and prices.

U.S. copper

***American Half Cents.* Cohen, Roger S.** Wigglesworth & Ghatt Co., Arlington, Va., 1982. Catalog listing of all known half cent varieties,

with photos accompanying
listings.

***America's Copper Coinage
1783-1857.*** American Numismatic Society, New York,
1985. Features articles about
state and federal copper coinage through the demise of the
large cent. Reprints of papers
presented at the ANS's 1984
Coinage of the Americas
Conference.

***Encyclopedia of United States
Half Cents 1793-1857.
Breen, Walter.*** American Institute of Numismatic Research, South Gate, Calif.,
1984. Historical information
and pedigrees, plus catalog
listing of all known half cent
varieties, with photos accompanying the listings.

The Fugio Cents. Kessler, Alan.
Colony Coin Co., Newtonville,
Mass. 1976. A catalog listing
of varieties of the United
States' first coinage, with
historical information.

Penny Whimsy. Sheldon, William H. Quarterman Publications Inc., Lawrence, Mass., 1983 (Reprint of 1958 edition, 1976 copyright). Catalog listing of known varieties of large cents from 1793 to 1814, with plates in back.

The Two-Cent Piece and Varieties. Kliman, Myron M. Sanford J. Durst Numismatic Publications, New York, 1983. Catalog listing of known varieties, with no photos.

United States Copper Cents 1816-1857. Newcomb, Howard R. Quarterman Publications Inc, Lawrence, Mass., 1981 (facsimile reprint of 1944 book). Catalog listing of known varieties of later large cents, with plates in back.

United States Copper Coins — An Action Guide for the Collector and Investor. Bowers and Merena Inc., Wolfeboro, N.H., 1984. Covers half cents, large cents, small cents and 2-cent pieces with historical information and investment advice.

U.S. silver

The Comprehensive Catalogue and Encyclopedia of U.S. Morgan and Peace Silver Dollars. **Van Allen, Leroy C., and Mallis, A. George.** Arco Publishing Co., New York, 1976. Historical information and catalog listing of all known varieties.

The Fantastic 1804 Dollar. **Bressett, Kenneth E., and Newman, Eric P.** Whitman Publishing Co., Racine, Wis., 1962. A numismatic mystery is solved in this in-depth study of the 1804 dollar, one of the United States' greatest rarities.

The United States Early Silver Dollars from 1794 to 1803. **Bolender, M.H.** Krause Publications, Iola, Wis., 1980. (Revised reprint of 1950 book.) Catalog listing of dollar varieties, with plates in back.

The United States Trade Dollar. **Willem, John M.** Sanford J. Durst Numismatic Publications, New York, 1983. Historical treatment of the Trade dollar, with mintage by month, varieties and rarity levels.

Early Half Dollar Varieties. **Overton, Al C.** Colorado Springs, Colo., 1970. Catalog listing of all known varieties, with photos accompanying listings.

The Walking Liberty Half Dollar. **Swiatek, Anthony.** Sanford J. Durst Numismatic Publications, New York, 1983. Catalog listing, with emphasis on distinguishing between strong strikes and weak strikes.

The Early Quarter Dollars of the United States. **Browning, A.W.** Sanford J. Durst Numismatic Publications, New York, 1977 (reprint of 1925 book). Catalog listing of known varieties, with plates at back.

Standing Liberty Quarters.
Cline, J.H. Cline's Rare Coins, Palm Harbor, Fla., 1986. Historical information, including correspondence between designer and Treasury officials, plus catalog listing and investment advice.

Encyclopedia of United States Liberty Seated Dimes.
Ahwash, Kamal M. Kamal Press, 1977. Catalog listing of known varieties, with over-sized photos accompanying listings.

***Early United States Dimes: 1796-1837.* Davis, David J.; Logan, Russell, J.; Lovejoy, Allen F.; McCloskey, John W.; Subjack, William L.** John Reich Collectors Society, 1984. Catalog of known varieties for Draped Bust and Capped Bust dimes, with over-sized photos accompanying listings.

The United States Half Dimes.
Valentine, Daniel W. Quarterman Publications Inc., Lawrence, Mass., 1975 (re-

print of 1931 book). Valentine catalog listing, plus updated information on other individuals.

U.S. gold

United States Gold Coins: An Illustrated History. **Bowers, Q. David.** Bowers and Ruddy Galleries, Los Angeles, 1982. The history of U.S. gold coins.

U.S. Gold Dollars through U.S. Double Eagles. **Akers, David W.** Paramount Publications, Englewood, Ohio, 1975-1982. A series of six books covering gold dollars, quarter eagles, $3 and $4 gold pieces, half eagles, eagles and double eagles; basically it records auction appearances by denomination, date and Mint mark.

United States Gold Patterns. **Akers, David W.** Paramount International Coin Corp., Englewood, Ohio, 1975. Subtitled "A photographic study of the gold patterns struck at the United States Mint from 1836 to 1907."

Tokens, medals

The Atwood-Coffee Catalogue of United States and Canadian Transportation Tokens. **Coffee Jr., John M., and Ford, Harold V.** The American Vecturist Association, Boston, 1983. The book catalogs mass transportation tokens and similar items, based on earlier Atwood systems and catalog. Other volumes catalog minor die varieties and record the history of the transportation token.

Early American Tokens, Hard Times Tokens, U.S. Merchant Tokens 1845-1860, United States Trade Tokens 1866-1889, Tokens of the Gay Nineties 1890-1900. **Rulau, Russell.** Krause Publications, Iola, Wis., 1981-1983. Five volumes in a planned series listing of all U.S. merchant tokens (except Civil War pieces) and related pieces in a soft-cover catalog format.

Medals of the United States Mint — The First Century 1792-1892. Julian, Robert W. Token and Medal Society Inc., 1977. Massive historical work covering all medallic works produced by the Mint during its first 100 years.

Patriotic Civil War Tokens. Fuld, George, and Fuld, Melvin. Civil War Token Society, 1982 (released 1984). Catalog lists all Civil War patriotic tokens, with historical information and chapters on related topics.

So-Called Dollars. Hibler, Harold E., and Kappen, Charles V. The Coin and Currency Institute, New York, 1963. Covers commemorative and exposition medals of near-dollar size in catalog format, listing metal varieties and historical information.

U.S. Civil War Store Cards. Fuld, George, and Fuld,

Melvin. Quarterman Publications, Lawrence, Mass., 1975. Catalogs all Civil War store cards by city and state, with historical information.

Video Arcade, Pinball, Slot Machine and Other Amusement Tokens of North America. **Alpert, Stephen A., and Smith, Kenneth E.** Amusement Token Collectors Association, Redondo Beach, Calif., 1984. Catalogs all known amusement tokens by state, province and miscellaneous categories.

Counterfeit detection

Counterfeit Detection. **Staff of the American Numismatic Association Certification Service**. American Numismatic Association, Colorado Springs, Colo., two volumes, 1983 and 1987. Reprints ANACS's columns appearing in *The Numismatist*, discussing and illustrating counterfeits and genuine specimens of dozens of U.S. coins, plus information about collectible varieties and ANACS procedures.

Counterfeits of U.S. States Coins. **Spanbauer, Larry.** Service Litho-Print Inc., Oshkosh, Wis., 1975. Illustrates many Colonial, private Mint and modern counterfeits and replicas.

Detecting Counterfeit Coins, Book 1. **Devine, "Lonesome" John.** Heigh Ho Printing Co., Newbury Park, Calif., Illustrates and describes many counterfeit U.S. minor and silver coins.

Detecting Counterfeit Gold Coins, Book 2. **Devine, "Lonesome" John.** Heigh Ho Printing Co., Newbury Park, Calif., 1977. Illustrates and describes many counterfeit gold coins.

Grading

The Accugrade System. **Hager, Alan.** Silver Dollars Unlimited Inc., Bedford, N.Y., 1984, Accugrade Inc., Greenwich, Conn., 1986. A three-volume guide to grading Uncirculated, Proof and prooflike Morgan, Peace and Eisenhower dollars.

Grading Coins: A Collection of Readings. **Edited by Bagg, Richard, and Jelinski, James J.** Essex Publications, Portsmouth, N.H., 1977. Collection of articles about grading from *The Numismatist, Whitman Numismatic Journal* and *Numismatic Scrapbook Magazine* from 1892 to 1976. Takes a historical approach.

A Guide to the Grading of United States Coins. **Brown, Martin T., and Dunn, John W.** General Distributors Inc., Denison, Texas, 1980. Uses line illustrations for U.S. coins in all denominations from half cent to double eagle in all grades.

NCI Grading Guide. **Halperin, James L.** Ivy Press, Dallas, Texas, 1986. Written by a principal grader of the Numismatic Certification Institute. Provides a step-by-step approach to the grading of

Uncirculated and Proof coins. Does not cover circulated grades.

New Photograde. **Ruddy, James F.** Bowers and Ruddy Galleries Inc., Los Angeles, 1972. Photographic guide to the grading of U.S. coins in all denominations from half cent to double eagle.

Official American Numismatic Association Grading Standards for United States Coins. **Bressett, Kenneth, and Kosoff, A.** Whitman Numismatic Products, Western Publishing, Racine, Wis., 1987. Official ANA guide to grading U.S. coins; third edition (1987) uses black-and-white photographs; first two editions use line illustrations. Includes non-illustrated guide to grading U.S. commemorative coins.

Errors, varieties

The Classification and Value of Errors on the Lincoln Cent. **Cohen, Jean.** Bonita Springs, Fla., 1969. Out of print. Illustrates through line drawings minor errors on Lincoln cents and lists their (outdated) values.

The Design Cud. **Marvin, Paul, and Margolis, Arnold.** Heigh Ho Printing Co., Newbury Park, Calif., 1979. In-depth explanation and photographs of how major die breaks, cuds, occur.

The Encyclopedia of Doubled Dies, Vols. 1 and 2. **Wexler, John A. Robert C.** Wilharm News Printing Co., Inc., Fort Worth, Texas, 1978 and 1981. Illustrates and describes doubled dies on U.S. coins, and how they occur.

How Error Coins are Made at the U.S. Mints. **Margolis, Arnold.** Heigh Ho Printing Co., Newbury Park, Calif., 1981. Describes and illustrates how coins are minted and how error coins occur.

Modern Mint Mistakes. **Steiner, Phillip, and Zimpfer, Michael.** Whispering Pines

Printing, Ind., 1975-1976. Provides general information and a price guide to error coins.

Official Price Guide to Mint Errors and Varieties. **Herbert, Alan.** House of Collectibles Inc., Orlando, Fla., 1981. Offers a general, overall look at error coins.

The RPM Book. **Wexler, John A., and Miller, Tom.** Lonesome John Publishing Co., Newbury Park, Calif., 1983. Describes and illustrates repunched and over Mint marks, with price information.

Paper money

Bureau of Engraving and Printing — The First Hundred Years 1862-1962. Sanford J. Durst Numismatic Publications, New York, 1978 (reprint of 1962 book published by the Treasury Department). Government history tracing history of BEP and government-issued paper money, postage stamps and revenue items.

***The Comprehensive Catalog of U.S. Paper Money*. Hessler, Gene.** BNR Press, Port Clinton, Ohio, 1983. Catalog listings of government issues, with historical information.

***The Encyclopedia of United States Fractional and Postal Currency*. Friedberg, Milton.** Numismatic and Antiquarian Service Corporation of America, Long Island, N.Y., 1978. Historical information and catalog of federal fractional notes of Civil War and Reconstruction.

***Military Payment Certificates*. Schwan, Fred**. BNR Press, Port Clinton, Ohio, 1981. Covers notes issued for use by military personnel stationed overseas from 1946 to 1973.

***Paper Money of the United States*. Friedberg, Robert.** The Coin and Currency Institute, Inc., Clifton, N.J., 1986.

Catalog listings, with numbering system that is used hobby-wide.

Standard Catalog of National Bank Notes. Hickman, John, and Oakes, Dean. Krause Publications, Iola, Wis., 1982. Lists 117,007 different national bank notes in catalog fashion, plus historical information.

Standard Handbook of Modern United States Paper Money. O'Donnell, Chuck. Krause Publications, Iola, Wis., 1982. For collectors of small-sized notes, with complete listings of all blocks and star blocks issued, varieties and quantities produced.

America's Currency 1789-1866. American Numismatic Society, New York, 1985. Examines paper money in the United States as issued by private issuers and local and state governments. Reprints papers presented at the 1985 Coinage of the Americas Conference.

Confederate and Southern States Currency. **Criswell, Grover C.** Grover C. Criswell's Publications, Florida, 1976. Covers all CSA issues, plus states issues of the Civil War.

The Early Paper Money of America. **Newman, Eric P.** Western Publishing Co., Racine, Wis., 1976. Covers all paper money issued by the Continental Congress, 13 original Colonies.

Society of Paper Money Collectors Wismer update series. The SPMC has published a series of catalogs of obsolete notes by state and territory. Books available from the SPMC include Rhode Island, Florida, Mississippi, Texas, Iowa, Minnesota, Alabama, Maine, Indiana, New Jersey, Vermont, Arkansas, Pennsylvania and a volume covering the Indian Territory, Oklahoma and Kansas.

Joining a club

One
Two
Three
Four
Five
Six

Belonging to your local coin club can put you in touch with people in your community with a mutual interest in one or more areas of numismatics.

Many collectors belong not only to local coin clubs, but also to state or regional coin clubs, associations devoted to a special collecting interests, the American Numismatic Association or international associations.

The question you might initially ask is, "Why do I need a club in the first place?"

Although many coin collectors are satisfied by pursuing the hobby alone, you may find it helpful and enjoyable sharing your experiences and knowledge at a local coin club meeting.

Collectors who have never belonged to a coin club before and beginning collectors may not even know a local coin club exists. Often, the local club will run a notice in the local newspaper announcing the date, time and location of its meetings.

Providing educational programs is the primary purpose of most clubs. Most of the programs are offered by the members themselves. In some instances, an experienced collector may be paired with a newcomer to coordinate a program, expanding everyone's knowledge.

EVEN BEGINNING COLLECTORS may have interesting stories to tell other club members.

Some clubs present programs using slide presentations and scripts prepared by members or slide/script programs prepared by numismatic organizations such as the American Numismatic Association, the Token and Medal Society and the Civil War Token Society.

Local clubs often conduct a coin auction after the meeting's regular program has been completed. In most cases, the coins and other numismatic items of-

Joining a club gives you access to other collectors' experience and knowledge.

fered for sale have been consigned or donated to the sale by the members. Depending on the size and geographic location of the club, the club may conduct one or more coin shows a year.

Clubs may also publish a bulletin or newsletter informing members of numismatic news and events. Such publications may also list the club's program schedule and recap activities from previous meetings.

Of some 2,000 clubs in the United States, probably no two are operated alike or have the same programs.

The *Coin World* Club Center

CLUBS RANGE in size from a few members to tens of thousands.

maintains information about many active clubs. Clubs wishing information about administration of a coin club can request secretary guidelines for keeping minutes, report forms, publicity outlines and membership cards.

Club presidents may request reprints for program aids, cards requesting samples of *Coin World*, information about fund-raising projects, and a variety of literature to hand out at coin shows or conventions.

Collectors can pick up tips from other collectors about how to put together a winning coin exhibit at a local, regional or national coin show or convention. Many collectors enjoy competing for the plaques, trophies and ribbons in exhibit competitions. Other collectors enjoy putting together non-competitive exhibits just to show what can be done.

Clubs planning coin shows may ask to be listed in the *Coin World* show calendar and for help in resolving conflicting dates with other clubs holding shows in their areas.

Collectors planning to visit or move to another city may inquire about the meeting dates and locations of coin clubs in that area.

All these services are available by writing Club Center, *Coin World*, Box 150, Sidney, Ohio 45365, telephone (513) 498-0800, ext. 242.

With roughly 30,000 members, the American Numismatic Association, referred to simply as the "ANA," is the world's largest numismatic organization. Now based in Colorado Springs, Colo., the ANA has its roots in Chicago.

In 1891, Dr. George Heath, publisher of *The Numismatist* (now the official ANA monthly magazine), announced in the August issue of that year that a

The American Numismatic Association supports many club activities throughout the country.

group of numismatists meeting in Chicago felt a need for an association. The ANA was born two months later.

ANA headquarters boasts a museum, which displays, on a rotating basis, exhibits consisting of numismatic items loaned or donated to the ANA.

The ANA Library, which began with two books, now boasts several thousand books, volumes, special catalogs and periodicals.

All material, with the exception of the library's collection of rare books and catalogs, may be borrowed by ANA members. Reprints of articles that have appeared in *The Numismatist* can also be requested.

The association maintains an audio-visual education program for clubs, a coin authentication and grading service, programs for young numismatists, numismatic training seminars and sponsors an annual National Coin Week program designed to promote numismatics.

The association also has a representative program that links representatives of individual clubs

ASK ABOUT BENEFITS of membership before joining a club.

with a regional coordinator.

For information about the ANA, write American Numismatic Association, 818 N. Cascade Ave., Colorado Springs, Colo. 80903; telephone (719) 632-2646.

Other national and regional coin associations, token and exonumia collectors organizations, organizations for paper money collectors and state associations:

Active Token Collectors Organization, 7411 Edledale Lane, Omaha, Neb. 68112.

Alabama Numismatic Society, Box 3601, West End Station, Birmingham, Ala. 35211.

American Medallic Sculpture Association, 431 Buena Vista Road, New City, N.Y. 10956.

American Numismatic Society, Broadway at 155th Street, New York, N.Y. 10032.

American Political Items Collectors, Box 340339, San Antonio, Texas, 78234.

American Society of Check Collectors, Route 2, Box 1, Iola, Wis. 54945.

American Tax Token Society, Box 614, Corvallis, Ore. 97339

American Vecturist Association, 46 Fenwood Drive, Old Saybrook, Conn. 06475.

Amusement Token Collectors Association, 328 Avenue F, Redondo Beach, Calif. 90277.

Arkansas Numismatic Society, 6600 Baseline Road, Little Rock, Ark. 72209.

Bank Token Society, Box 383, Newtonville, Mass. 02160.

Blue Ridge Numismatic Association, 1501 Akins Drive, Chattanooga, Tenn. 37411.

Bond & Share Society, Box 120, Station K, Montreal, Quebec, Canada H1N 3K9.

Bust Nut Half Club, Box 4875, Margate, Fla. 33063.

California Association of Token Collectors, 516 W. 99th St., Los Angeles, Calif. 90044.

California Exonumist Society, Box 6599, San Diego, Calif. 92106.

California State Numismatic Association, Box 63, Upland, Calif. 91786.

Central States Numismatic Society, Box 223, Hiawatha, Iowa, 52233.

Civil War Token Society, Box 3412, Lake Mary, Fla. 32746.

Club of Illinois Numismatists, 2813 W. 85th Place, Chicago, Ill. 60652.

Colorado-Wyoming Numismatic Association, 519 W. Mountain Ave., Fort Collins, Colo. 80521.

Combined Organizations of Numismatic Error Collectors of America, Box 915, Palo Alto, Calif. 94302.

Currency Club of Chester County, Pa., 420 Owen Road, West Chester, Pa. 19380.

Dedicated Wooden Money Collectors, 1028 Azalea Court, La Marque, Texas 77568.

Early American Coppers, Box 15782, Cincinnati, Ohio 45215.

Empire State Numismatic Association, Rt. 2, Box 247, Troy, N.Y. 12182.

Essay Proof Society, Route 4, Colonial Drive, Katonah, N.Y. 10536.

Florida Token Society, Box 1091, Lake Alfred, Fla. 33850.

Florida United Numismatists, Box 2256, Clearwater, Fla. 34617.

Franklin Half Dollar Collectors Consortium, Box 6663, San Pedro, Calif. 90734.

Garden State Numismatic Association, Box 3462, Toms River, N.J. 08756.

Georgia Numismatic Association, Box 611, Lilburn, Ga. 30247.

Georgia State Token-Exonumia Association, Box 3412, Lake Mary, Fla. 32746.

Great Eastern Numismatic Association, 490 Green Hill Lane, Berwyn, Pa. 19312.

Hawaii State Numismatic Association, Box 477, Honolulu, Hawaii 96809.

Illinois Numismatic Association, 116 Cooper Drive, New Lenox, Ill. 60451.

Indiana State Numismatic Association, Box 44337, Indianapolis, Ind. 46204.

Indiana-Kentucky-Ohio Token & Medal Society, Box 192, Dayton, Ohio 45449.

International Bank Note Society, Box 1642, Racine, Wis. 53401.

International Organization of Wooden Money Collectors, Box 395, Goose Creek, S.C. 29445.

Iowa Numismatic Association, Box 65356, W. Des Moines, Iowa 50265.

John Reich Collectors Society, Box 205, Ypsilanti, Mich. 48197.

Kansas Numismatic Association, Rt. 3, Box 5, Chanute, Kan. 66720.

Kentucky State Numismatic Association, 1318 E. Breckinridge, Louisville, Ky. 40204.

Liberty Seated Collectors Club, Box 1062, Midland, Mich. 48641.

Louisiana Numismatic Society, Box 897, Opelousas, La. 70571.

Love Token Society, Box 59699, Chicago, Ill. 60659.

Maine Numismatic Association, Box H, Brunswick, Maine 04011.

Maryland State Numismatic Association, Box 6533, Sparrows Point, Md. 21219.

Maryland Token & Medal Society, Box 3273, Baltimore, Md. 21228.

Michigan State Numismatic Society, Box 1157, Battle Creek, Mich. 49016.

Middle Atlantic Numismatic Association, Box 787, Pearl River, N.Y. 10965.

Midwest Numismatic Association, 9723 Marsh, Kansas City, Mo. 64134.

Minnesota Organization of Numismatists, Box 565, Rochester, Minn. 55903.

Mississippi Numismatic Association, Box 13525, Jackson, Miss. 39236.

Missouri Numismatic Society, 5005 S. Grand Blvd., St. Louis, Mo. 63111.

National Scrip Collectors Association, Box 29, Fayetteville, W. Va. 25840.

Nebraska Numismatic Association, Box 683, Sutherland, Neb. 69165.

New England Numismatic Association, Box 99, W. Roxbury, Mass. 02132.

New Hampshire Numismatic Association, Box 1655, Dover, N.H. 03820.

New Jersey Exonumia Society, Box 363, Cranford, N.J. 07016.

New Jersey Numismatic Society, Box 67, Wharton, N.J. 07885.

New York State Wooden Money Society, 25 N. Wayne Ave., West Haverstraw, N.Y. 10993.

North Carolina Numismatic Association, Box 20653, Greensboro, N.C. 27420.

Northern California Numismatic Association, Box 4104, Vallejo, Calif. 94590.

Numismatic Association of Southern California, Box 5173, Buena Park, Calif. 90622.

Numismatic Bibliomania Society, 4223 Iraquis, Lakewood, Calif. 90713.

Numismatists of Wisconsin, Box 155, Mazomanie, Wis. 53560.

Oklahoma Numismatic Association, Box 18753, Oklahoma City, Okla. 73154.

Old Timer Assay Commission Society, 3070 S. Franklin, Denver, Colo. 80210.

Oregon Numismatic Society, 4144 S.E. Clinton, Portland, Ore. 97202.

Pacific Coast Numismatic Society, 610 Arlington Ave., Berkeley, Calif. 94707.

Pacific Northwest Numismatic Association, 20121 1st Ave. S., Seattle, Wash. 98198.

Paper Money Collectors of Michigan, Box 163, Victor, N.Y. 14564.

Penn-Ohio Coin Clubs, 612 White St., Toledo, Ohio 43605.

Pennsylvania Association of Numismatists, Box 144, Pittsburgh, Pa. 15230.

Society for U.S. Commemorative Coins, 14252 Culver, Apt. 490, Irvine, Calif. 92714.

Society of Bearded Numismatists, Box 970218, Miama, Fla. 33197.

Society of Lincoln Cent Collectors, Box 5465, N. Hollywood, Calif. 91616.

Society of Paper Money Collectors, Box 1085, Florissant, Mo. 63031.

Society of Philatelists and Numismatists, 1929 Millis St., Montebello, Calif. 90640.

Society of Ration Token Collectors, Box J, Baltimore, Md. 21228.

South Carolina Numismatic Association, Box 12163, Columbia, S.C.

South Dakota Coin & Stamp Association, 106 W. 5th, Pierre, S.D. 57501.

Souvenir Card Collectors Society, Box 4155, Tulsa, Okla. 74159.

Tennessee State Numismatic Society, Box 80052, Chattanooga, Tenn. 37411.

Texas Numismatic Association, 2901 Silverleaf Drive, Austin, Texas 78757.

The Elongated Collectors, Box 161, Fenton, Mich. 48430.

Token and Medal Society, Box 3412, Lake Mary, Fla. 32746.

Utah Numismatic Society, Box 15054, Salt Lake City, Utah 84115.

Virginia Numismatic Association, 3902 Rose Lane, Annandale, Va. 22003.

World's Fair Collectors Society, Box 20806, Sarasota, Fla. 34238.

Guide to terms

Following are definitions of terms that appear in **bold type** throughout the book. Following each description is a reference to the page or pages where the term appears with the most meaningful context. Capitalization of some terms in numismatics may affect their meaning. The following are capitalized according to the style adopted by *Coin World*.

8 reales — Spanish silver coin popular at the time of American Independence, it was the model for the American silver dollar. These coins are sometimes associated with pirate treasures, and may be referred to as "pieces of eight." *Page 39*

About Good — Grading term. *Page 82*

About Uncirculated — Grading term. *Page 81*

altered coin — A coin that has been tampered with, usually in an attempt to make it appear rare or valuable. *Page 74*

annealing — A process of controlled heating and cooling of metal, annealing softens planchets for striking. *Page 46*

anvil die — In modern coin production, this is the bottom die, or the die fixed in position. The term is derived from the early days of coinage, when lumps of metal were placed on an anvil and struck with a hammer. *Page 42*

assay — To determine the precious metal content of a metal ore or alloy. *Page 43*

barter — Trade, especially trading goods or services for other goods or services in the absence of money. *Page 31*

bit — In Colonial America, the Spanish silver 8 reales coin was popular. This coin was sometimes cut into eight pieces for small change. Each piece was called a bit. When the United States modeled its silver dollar on the 8 reales, a bit referred to one-eighth of a dollar, or 12-1/2 cents. *Page 39*

bourse — Rhymes with "horse." At a coin show or convention, the bourse is the area where dealers set up tables of collectibles to sell. *Page 24*

circulate, circulation — The movement of money in an economy. Money is passed from person to person. Circulating coins are distinct from coins produced for collectors or investors. *Page 33*

clad coins — Generally refers to United States dime, quarter dollar, half dollar and dollar coins produced since 1965. These have layers of silver-colored copper-nickel bonded to a copper core. Clad coins replaced expensive silver coins in circulation. Other materials may be used for clad coins. *Page 14, 40*

coining press — The machine used to impress the image on pieces of metal to make coins. The coining press is one step of a long process in coin production. *Page 49*

collar — A ring of metal that contains the coin being struck in the coining press. The collar prevents metal from squeezing out from between the dies, and also may be used to place simple designs, such as reeding, on a coin's edge. *Page 50*

color — When coin collectors refer to a coin's color, they are refering to how it compares to its original appearance. Copper cents, for instance, when new are referred to as "red." When they age, they may become "brown." *Page 66*

commemorative coins — Coins struck to honor a person, event or place. These are usually produced in limited quantities for collectors, but they may also be placed into circulation, like the Bicentennial of American Independence quarter dollars, half dollars and dollars dated 1776-1976. *Page 26*

contact mark — Sometimes called a "bag mark," a contact mark is a scar or blemish on the surface of a coin. These are caused by normal handling of coins even before they reach circulation. *Page 63*

counterfeit — Counterfeits may be coins or paper money. They are produced with the intent to deceive or defraud. Some counterfeits are made to pass as circulating money, while others are intended to appear as valuable rarities. *Page 73*

debased — Money that becomes less valuable. When precious metals such as gold and silver were used in coins, over time, less pure metal was used in coins of the same denomination. The coins would buy less, because they were worth less. *Page 34*

die — A metal punch that impresses an image onto the surface of a coin. *Page 47*

dipped, dipping — Cleaning coins by placing them into a solvent. Dipping usually dissolves some of the coin's surface, making it artificially bright, but lacking in eye appeal. *Page 67, 90*

edge — The edge is the part of the coin that separates the obverse from the reverse. It can be smooth or may have some design. It is best to hold coins in your collection by the edge. *Page 5*

encapsulated coin — A coin that has been sealed into a plastic holder, usually after it has been graded by a grading service. *Page 71*

Extremely Fine — Grading term. *Page 81, 83*

eye appeal — The quality that makes a coin attractive. The precise definition of eye appeal differs with each individual. *Page 69*

face value — The value that is expressed on a piece of money, or its intended value by the issuer, such as "quarter dollar," "one cent," or "10 dollars." *Page 34*

fiat — A currency, or money system, that is not backed by precious metal reserves. *Page 36*

Fine — Grading term. *Page 82, 84*

Fleur de Coin — Grading term. *Page 85*

flip — A coin holder, usually a plastic one that has two pouches, one to hold a coin and the other to hold identification of the piece. It is folded over, or "flipped," to close. *Page 93*

flow lines — Microscopic lines in the surface metal of a coin. As light is reflected off flow lines, it produces a soft glow known as luster. Coins that are circulated or that have been harshly cleaned have their flow lines removed, and therefore little luster. *Page 65*

Fugio cents — The first coinage authorized by the new United States government in 1787. They were privately struck, but under federal inspection. *Page 39*

Good — Grading term. *Page 82, 85*

grade, grading — Grading is the act of determining the condition of a coin or other collectible. The grade is a number or phrase representative of the condition. *Page 61*

grading service — An organization that assigns grades to collectible items, usually for a fee. *Page 70*

half disme — Pronounced "half deem," this 1792 silver coin with a face value of 5 cents is believed to be the first coinage struck by the United States Mint. *Page 40*

hammer die — In modern coin production, it is the die that moves in the coining press. It is derived from the days when coinage was struck with a hammer. *Page 42*

hammer price — In an auction, this is the price the auctioneer calls the winning bid. The hammer price does not include buyer's fees or any other additional charges that the buyer may eventually pay for an auction lot. *Page 22*

hologram — A three-dimensional image. Some countries are experimenting with using holograms in their paper money as a security measure against counterfeiting. *Page 59*

hub — A positive-image metal punch used to make mirror-image dies. *Page 49.*

inflation, inflationary — In economics, when the same amount of money buys less over time. Inflation is why a car cost $3,000 in 1968, while a comparable car costs $10,000 in 1988. *Page 35*

intaglio — Intaglio is a method of printing that involves engraved metal plates. The paper is forced under high pressure into the ink-filled engraved lines of the plate. United States Federal Reserve notes are printed by the intaglio method as a measure against counterfeiting. *Page 55*

intrinsic value — The value of a coin's metal content, regardless of its face value. *Page 34*

legal tender — Money that has the official approval of a governing body. *Page 37*

legal tender bullion coin — Government-issued precious metal coins produced for investors, they have legal tender status, and usually a nominal face value, even though they are not intended to circulate as currency. *Page 37*

luster — The soft glow of a well-preserved coin, luster is the result of light reflecting off of microscopic flow lines in the metal. *Page 64*

master die — A metal punch used to produce "working hubs," which are then used to produce "working dies." *Page 49*

master hub — A metal punch used to produce "master dies." *Page 49*

medals — Collectible numismatic items, usually made from metal, that are commemorative or artistic. Some medals are produced by methods similar to coin production. Some medals are official government issues, but are not legal tender. *Page 7*

Mediocre — Grading term. *Page 85*

Mint State — Grading term. *Page 62, 80*

New, Uncirculated — Paper money grading term. *Page 83*

numismatics, numismatist — The broad term covering the study of money or money-like items. A numismatist is more deeply involved in research and study than a "collector." *Page 6*

obsolete paper money — Paper money issued prior to 1865 by banks that are no longer operating. The term "broken bank note" will sometimes be used, although not all banks that issued these notes closed because of failure. *Page 12*

obverse — On coins, the front or face; "heads." Usually the side with the dominant design. *Page 5*

overprinting — In the production of United States Federal Reserve notes, the main designs are printed on the face and back. Then the serial numbers and Federal Reserve seals are "overprinted" in a separate process. *Page 57*

paper money — Printed monetary instruments. Modern collectors may be challenged for a new term as nations experiment with plastics and other materials for their printed money. Some collectors incorrectly use the term "bank notes" to refer to all paper money, or the term "currency" to refer to only paper money. Currency may also be coin. *Page 35*

patina — The surface quality that a coin acquires over time as the metal reacts with the environment. *Page 90*

planchet — Sometimes called a blank or flan, it is a piece of metal formed and ready to be struck into coinage, but not yet impressed with the coin design. *Page 44*

polyvinylchloride, PVC — A chemical found in some soft, pliable plastic coin or paper money holders. PVC degrades into a particularly ugly and damaging goo. Storage devices containing PVC should be avoided. *Page 94*

Poor — Grading term. *Page 85*

Proof — Sometimes used as a grading term, especially with a number, such as "Proof 65." Technically, it is a method of manufacture using great care to produce special collectibles. In paper money circles, a proof (lowercase p) is a test printing before a production run. *Page 80*

Proof set — Generally a representative sample of the coins produced by a nation for circulation, but manufactured and packaged specifically for collectors. Some Proof sets may be privately assembled and packaged. *Page 27*

reeding — The ridges on the edge of a coin. *Page 50*

replica — A copy or reproduction of a numismatic item. *Page 74*

reverse — The back of a coin; "tails." Usually the secondary design side. *Page 5*

riddlers — Vibrating screens that sort out non-standard planchets. *Page 45*

rim — The raised ridge around the obverse and reverse of a coin. The rim's function is to protect the surface and help in stacking. The term is sometimes confused with "edge." *Page 47*

screw press — Early hand-operated machine for striking coins. The operator swung a weighted arm that turned a screw, which then pressed the die into the planchet. More accurate than hand-hammering. *Page 41*

silver certificates — Paper money issued by the United States, they could be redeemed for silver until the mid-1960s. No longer produced, they are still legal tender, but cannot be redeemed for silver. *Page 36*

slab — Popular nickname for certain kinds of coin encapsulation methods, especially those that are permanently sealed and rectangular. *Page 71, 95*

souvenir cards — Popular collectible items, souvenir cards are usually well-printed on heavy paper using an engraving used on paper money. They also contain some information of a historic or commemorative nature. *Page 7*

specie — Usually precious metal coins in circulation valued at their precious metal content. Paper money that can be redeemed in coin is specie currency. *Page 36*

strike — The act of impressing the image of a die into a planchet, making a coin. The quality of strike is important when determining a coin's condition and value. *Page 65*

strip — Rolls of coinage metal to be punched into planchets. *Page 44*

surcharge — An extra charge placed on an item, the revenue from a surcharge is usually earmarked for a specific fund. It has been the recent practice of the United States Congress to place a surcharge on commemorative coins either to benefit a worthy organization, or to be used to reduce the national debt. *Page 26*

tokens — Coin-like money substitutes, generally privately issued. Tokens have played an important part in the economy of the United States during periods when small change was difficult to obtain. *Page 6*

toning — As the metal in a coin reacts with its environment, it may produce varying shades of color. Toning can be very attractive or very ugly. How it affects the value of a coin is a matter of personal taste. *Page 66*

Uncirculated — Technically, a coin or note that has never been used. Grading term. *Page 62, 80, 83*

Uncirculated Mint set — Usually a representative set of a nation's circulating coinage that has been specially packaged for collectors, but not so elaborate as a Proof set. *Page 27*

upsetting mill — A machine that squeezes planchets so that they have a raised rim, in preparation for striking into coins. *Page 47*

Very Fine — Grading term. *Page 82, 84*

Very Good — Grading term. *Page 82, 84*

vignettes — Small scenes engraved on paper money. Sometimes produced for collectors as "vignette sheets." The term derives from the fact that many scenes on paper money are details of larger paintings. *Page 7*

watermark — When paper is manufactured, it is possible to slightly vary the thickness in certain areas and produce a design. These designs will appear as shadowy when the paper is held up to the light. It is useful in paper money as a security measure against counterfeiting. *Page 59*

Wheat Ear cent — Lincoln cent produced from 1909-1958, the name comes from the two stalks of wheat on the reverse of the coins. *Page 14*

working die — A metal punch that is used to impress images into coins. *Page 49*

working hub — A metal punch used to produce "working dies." *Page 49*